Frontispiece: William Cuningham, From *The Cosmographical Glasse*

Front Cover: [8] 1629 (1646) Pieter Verbiest

By permission of the British Library, Maps d.177.d.1.(11) (detail)

The Printed Plans of Norwich 1558-1840

A Carto-Bibliography

Raymond Frostick

Published by Raymond Frostick, Norwich, England.
ISBN 0 9542471 0 8
© Raymond Frostick 2002
Printed in England by Witley Press Limited Hunstanton, Norfolk

CONTENTS

Page

Abbreviations vi
Preface vii
Introduction ix
Illustrations - Plates 1-4 xiii

THE PRINTED PLANS OF NORWICH 1558 - 1840

1.	1558	William **Cunningham**	1
2.	1581	Georg **Braun** and Franz **Hogenberg**	4
3.	1591	Francisco **Valezo**	7
4.	1611	John **Speed** (Plate 1)	8
5.	1617	Jodocus **Hondius** (Junior) (1)	9
6.	c.1623	Claes Janszoon **Visscher**	10
7.	1625	Jodocus **Hondius** (Junior) (2)	11
8.	1629	Pieter **Verbiest**	12
9.	1631	Daniel **Meisner**	13
10.	1661	Rutger **Hermannides**	15
11.	1662	Peter **Stent**	16
12.	1665	Christopher **Saxton**	16
13.	c.1666	John **Speed** (Plate 2)	17
14.	1668	Robert **Walton**	18
15.	1690	Johann Christoph **Beer**	19
16.	1696	Thomas **Cleer** (1)	20
17.	1696	Thomas **Cleer** (2)	23
18.	1706	Vincenzo **Coronelli** (1)	23
19.	1706	Vincenzo **Coronelli** (2)	24
20.	c.1710	Sutton **Nicholls**	25
21.	1728	John **Hoyle**	27
22.	1723	Thomas **Kirkpatrick** (N.E. Prospect)	29
23.	1723	Thomas **Kirkpatrick** (Plan)	33
24.	1725	Norwich **Gazette** (N.E. Prospect)	34
25.	1726	Norwich **Mercury** (N.E. Prospect)	35
26.	1727	James **Corbridge** (Plan)	36
27.	1730	James **Corbridge** (N.E. Prospect)	38
28.	1731	Thomas **Goddard** and William **Chase** (N.E. Prospect)	39
29.	1739	George **Foster** (N.E. Prospect)	40
30.	1740	Thomas **Goddard** and Robert **Goodman** (N.E. Prospect)	41
31.	1741	Samuel and Nathaniel **Buck** (N.E. Prospect)	42
32.	1741	Samuel and Nathaniel **Buck** (S.E. Prospect)	44
33.	1746	Francis **Blomefield** (1)	44
34.	1753	John **Hinton** (S.E. Prospect)	47

35.	1765	John **Ryland** (S.E. Prospect)	49
36.	1766	Samuel **King** (1)	50
37.	1766	Samuel **King** (2)	52
38.	1768	Martin **Booth** (N.E. Prospect)	53
39.	1768	Cluer **Dicey** (N. E. Prospect)	53
40.	1774	Robert **Goadby** (S.E Prospect)	54
41.	1779	John **Thompson**	55
42.	1781	Marcus **Armstrong** (N.E. Prospect)	57
43.	1783	Thomas **Smith**	59
44.	1789	Anthony **Hochstetter**	59
45.	1791	**Political Magazine** (S.E. Prospect)	61
46.	1802	John **Ninham**	62
47.	1806	Francis **Blomefield** (2)	63
48.	1807	George **Cole**	63
49.	1809	Harold Aston **Barker**	66
50.	1819	Thomas **Starling**	66
51.	1821	Richard **Taylor** (1)	67
52.	1821	Richard **Taylor** (2)	68
53.	1830	William Salter **Millard** and Joseph **Manning**	68
54.	1832	Robert Kearsley **Dawson** (O.S.)	71
55.	c.1834	Joseph **Manning**	73
56.	1834	William **Pinnock**	73
57.	1835	**Kemp** and **Nichols**	75
58.	1835	R. **Creighton**	76
59.	1836	William **Ionn**	77
60.	1837	Robert Kearsley **Dawson** (Large)	77
61.	1837	Robert Kearsley **Dawson** (Small)	78
62.	1838	**Ordnance Survey**	78

Select Bibliography 80

Index 81

Abbreviations

BL	British Library, London
Bod	Bodleian Library, Oxford
Castle	Norwich Castle Museum, Historic Maps Collection
CUL	Cambridge University Library
DNB	Dictionary of National Biography
Nfk. Lib.	Norfolk Heritage Centre, Norfolk and Norwich Millennium Library, Norwich
NRO	Norfolk Record Office
PRO	Public Record Office
RCF	Author's collection

Works which have been regulary cited in the text may be found in the Bibliography, under the surname of the author, and the appropriate date.

PREFACE

This book lists the printed plans of Norwich from 1558 to 1840, and it is not intended to be a history of the city. Plans, however, are an important source of information for the serious historian, as well as providing never ending fascination for the general reader. The only comprehensive book of reference on Norwich plans was written over seventy years ago, copies are now difficult to find, and in the intervening years information has come to light which means that it is now in need of substantial revision.

As a native of Norfolk, and having spent a major part of my working life in Norwich, I have always been fascinated by the history of the county and of the city as shown by their maps and plans. I have had the advantage of being able to study those held by the Norfolk Heritage Centre in the Norfolk and Norwich Millennium Library in Norwich, (most of which escaped the library fire of 1994), and those in the Norwich Castle Museum. Also over the years I have been able to acquire my own considerable collection. It has been my intention for some time to update the published information, and in this work I have endeavoured to do so in respect of Norwich plans. I hope that I may subsequently do likewise in respect of the earlier printed maps of the county.

The most important local public collections of Norwich plans are those of the Norfolk Heritage Centre, and of the Castle Museum. I have indicated by a footnote to each of the plans where copies are held, and I have also referred to those in my own collection, which can be made available for inspection on request. For most of the plans I have also given references for the British Library, where many of the plans are to be found in the King's Topographical collection in the Map Library, and with the Dawson Turner Manuscripts, and also for the Bodleian at Oxford, principally for those in the Gough collection. In addition, for certain of the rarer plans references have been given for copies in the Cambridge University Library and the Public Record Office.

I am particularly grateful for the encouragement received from the Norfolk Library and Information Service, and for the help given by the Norfolk Heritage Centre, the Castle Museum, and the staff of the British Library and the Bodleian. I am also pleased to acknowledge, advice and information from a number of individuals, including Christopher Barringer, Philip Burden, David Cubitt, Ron Fiske, Ralph Hyde, Donald Hodson, Roger Kain, Valerie Scott, Peter Pank, David Smith, Clive Wilkins-Jones and Laurence Worms. My thanks to Terence Burchall for the photography for many of the illustrations.

Finally I thank the following for permission to include these illustrations: the British Library, Numbers [8], [14] and [20]; Cambridge University Library, Number [55]; the Norfolk Heritage Centre, the Frontispiece, and Numbers [1], [3], [24], [25], [29], and [53]; Norwich Castle Museum, Number 59; Ron Fiske, Number [35]. Other illustrations are taken from my own collection.

There will undoubtedly be errors and omissions in a work of this kind, and for these I accept full responsibility. I would be pleased to receive a note of any corrections or additions, and will ensure that they are added to the reference copy of the book which will be held by the Norfolk Heritage Centre in Norwich.

Norwich 2002

INTRODUCTION

General Background

In the middle of the sixteenth century Norwich was one of the principal provincial cities of England, with a growing sense of civic pride and of civic power, and it was even described in a contemporary publication as 'not unworthy of being compared to London'.[1] Of course London as the capital city always remained pre-eminent in size of population and importance, but Norwich had an early reputation as 'A Fine City', and as the cultural and economic centre of one of the most highly populated areas of the country. Following the Industrial Revolution in the eighteenth century, the rapid growth of the towns of the Midlands and the North makes it easy to overlook the earlier urban supremacy of cities such as Norwich, Bristol and York.

It is not altogether surprising, therefore, that Norwich has a special place in the story of English urban mapping, as does Norfolk in the history of the mapping of the English counties. The plan of the city in 1558 by William Cuningham **[1]** is the earliest surviving printed map of known date of any English town,[2] while Christopher Saxton's map of Norfolk of 1574 is the first printed map of a single English county.

This carto-bibliography is intended to list and briefly describe the printed plans and principal prospects of Norwich from 1558 to 1840.[3] Any end date must be in a sense arbitrary, but by the early years of Victorian England maps and plans were beginning to proliferate. The development of lithographic printing made it easier for publishers to amend and revise, made all the more necessary as the growth of the railways began to change the face of the countryside; the railway did not finally arrive in Norwich until 1844. Moreover with the publication of detailed large scale plans such as that of Millard and Manning in 1830 **[53]**, and the issue by the Ordnance Survey of its one inch series covering Norwich in 1838 **[62]**, the mapping scene was fundamentally changing.[4] The story of plans of Norwich after 1840 will have to be kept for another occasion.

Plans, Bird's-Eye Views, and Prospects

A feature of early urban mapping was the 'bird's-eye view', whereby a realistic impression of the town was given by depicting the streets and buildings as they might be viewed if one could look down from above (e.g.Cuningham **[1]**); similarly a 'prospect' may be taken from some viewpoint outside the town itself (e.g. Kirkpatrick **[22]**). These prospects may not be thought to be 'plans' as the word is usually understood nowadays, but where the intention of the artist or surveyor is to give an impression of the town as a whole it seems appropriate to refer to them. I have followed the precedent set by Stephen (see below) in including the few most important prospects of the city, those of Kirkpatrick and of the Bucks **[31]** and **[32]**, and those derived directly from them. The more general views of the city, of which one finds an increasing number towards the end of the 18th century, are outside the scope of this work.[5]

Earlier Lists of Norwich Plans

The most comprehensive list of Norwich plans is *Descriptive List of Norwich Plans and the Principal Early Views 1541-1914,* by the then City Librarian, George Stephen, printed together with *A Descriptive List of the Printed Maps of Norfolk 1574-1916* by Thomas Chubb, published in Norwich in 1928.The whole work is usually referred to simply as 'Chubb', but the parts relating to Norwich plans and Norfolk maps are separately referred to throughout this work as

'Stephen' and 'Chubb' respectively.

Stephen was able to base his work on the collections in the Norwich Public Library, most of which still exist, and in the Map Library of what was then the British Museum. Earlier listing of Norwich plans, to which Stephen will doubtless have had access, include the following -

a. Richard Gough's *British Topography,* published in London in 1780. Norfolk maps and Norwich plans are referred to in the opening section of Volume 2. Many of the maps and plans were in Gough's own collection, and are now in the Gough Collection in the Bodleian in Oxford.

b. *The Norfolk Topographers Manual,* with an Index of the Drawings etc, inserted in a copy of Blomefield's *History of Norfolk* in the Library of Dawson Turner at Yarmouth, ed. W.C.Ewing, London and Norwich, 1842, pp. 103-4 and Appendix pp.95-6. The Dawson Turner collections are now in the British Library, indexed as Additional Manuscripts.

c. *Early Maps of Norwich,* described by W.T Bensley, a section in *The Streets and Lanes of the City of Norwich* by John Kirkpatrick, edited by W Hudson, Norwich, and published by the Norfolk and Norwich Archaeological Society in 1889. Dr. Bensley's Article was separately published as *Early Maps of the City of Norwich* in Norwich in 1890.

d. *A Rough Catalogue of Maps Relating to Norwich and Norfolk* by Harry Brittain, in *The Norfolk Antiquarian Miscellany, Second Series, Part 1,* Norwich 1906, pp.114 ff.

Current Literature

In recent years there has been a great upsurge of interest in early mapping, with many books both for the expert and the interested collector. There is a growing number of carto-bibliographies of maps of the English counties, but comparatively little has been published about the mapping of individual English towns and cities.[6] With the exception of London,[7] such information is mainly confined to local and other society journals which may not be readily accessible to the general reader; it is hoped therefore that this list of Norwich plans, particularly of those published in the 16th and 17th centuries, may be of relevance to the study of the mapping of other provincial towns.

Norwich Plans on Norfolk Maps

A number of Norwich plans are found as insets on maps of the county of Norfolk, of which probably the best known is that of John Speed **[4]**. Chubb's *Descriptive List* of the county maps now requires substantial revision. Where, therefore, the Norwich plan is part of a county map, and where the plan remains unchanged, I have not generally referred in detail to different editions of the map. However, where a Norwich plan is an inset on maps other than those of the county, (e.g. Hondius **[7]**), different editions of the map have been described.

What is Meant by Norwich ?

Most of the Norwich plans listed here are of the city as bounded by the city walls. Apart from the small suburbs of Heigham and Pockthorpe, development outside the walls was very limited until the end of the 18th century, by which time the gates and large sections of the walls had been removed. However when Cuningham drew his plan in 1558 the boundaries of the city, or more correctly the 'county of the city', had already been defined to include a much larger area.[8] The city's second charter of Henry IV in 1404 stated that the city should be separated from the county of Norfolk, and as a county itself should be called 'the county of the city of Norwich'. There remained, however, some uncertainty as to the exact boundaries, which were finally defined in detail in the charter of Philip and Mary in 1556.[9] This confirmed that the hamlets of Eaton,

Earlham, Catton, Thorpe, Trowse Millgate and Lakenham, together with the river to Hardley Cross, were within the the outer boundaries of the city. However it was not until the 19th century, with the plans of Dawson [54], Manning [55], Kemp and Nichols [57], Creighton [58] and Ionn [59], that these outer boundaries are shown on any of the listed plans.[10] These boundaries remained substantially unchanged until the local government reorganisation in 1974, when Norwich lost its status as a county borough, and became a district within the county of Norfolk.

An Overview of the Norwich Plans

The list includes 62 plans, but it will be seen that these are derived from a comparatively small number of original drawings or surveys. Copying by one publisher from another was commonplace during most of the period under consideration, usually without acknowledgment of source. The first, the outstandingly important plan of William Cuningham [1], set the scene for almost 150 years. Of the 17 plans listed from the 16th and 17th centuries all except the last two, those of Thomas Cleer [16] and [17], can be traced directly to his pioneering work, and his influence extends into the beginning of the 18th century with the curious plans of Coronelli [18] and [19]. Many of these are of decorative rather than of cartographic interest, but their appearance is an indication of the importance of Norwich during this period.

Cleer's plans mark a turning point in the story of the mapping of the city. For the first time they are the work of a professional surveyor, providing the first scale plans of the city. They also mark a significant change in printing and publication. Cuningham's *Cosmographical Glasse* was written in Norwich and printed in London, but almost all the plans which were derived from his work were engraved or published not in England but on the continent, in cities which include Cologne, Frankfurt, Nuremberg, Venice, Padua, and in what became the centre of map making during the 17th century, Amsterdam. The publication of town plans, particularly in Germany and the Netherlands, became popular in a way which did not happen in England; in addition to Braun and Hogenberg's great *Civitates Orbis Terrarum* [2], major works included the numerous editions of Munster's *Cosmographia*, the plans of Merian, and the town books of Blaeu, Deventer and Jansson. Only the publication of the town plans in Speed's *Theatre* [4] can in any way be comparable to what was happening on the continent, but they were included as incidental to the maps of their counties, and they were engraved, not in England, but in Amsterdam.

After the final appearance of the plans of Coronelli in 1706, all the plans of Norwich in this list were published either in London or in Norwich itself. Printing in Norwich was revived, and with it the publication of the local newspapers [24] and [25], and John Hoyle [21] appears as the first of a number of local engravers. The plans were increasingly local productions, to be included in local histories and directories, e.g. Blomefield [33], Thompson [41] and Smith [43], or as separate publications for the local community e.g. King [36] and Hochstetter [44].

In the period between Cleer in 1696 and Hochstetter in 1789 the influence of Cleer is seen very clearly in the smaller plans e.g. Nicholls [20] and Hoyle [21]. His presentation of the city was also substantially followed in the larger scale plans of Corbridge [26] and Blomefield [33]; however both of these are important in their own right, the former, a professional surveyor, including drawings of many of the city's buildings, and the latter, as a dedicated historian, adding to his plan much detailed information. As we move into the second half of the 18th century another professional surveyor, Samuel King, produced a very competent and large scale plan in 1766 [36], but by far the most important plan was that of Anthony Hochstetter in 1789 [44]. Another professional surveyor, Hochstetter set a new standard in urban mapmaking for the city, issuing much the most detailed plan to date. It was another 40 years before anything comparable was to be produced.

The early years of the 19th century saw the inclusion of plans of Norwich in a number of national publications, Cole **[48]**, Starling **[50]**, Pinnock **[56]** and Creighton **[58]**, and a variety of styles in the interesting works of Barker **[49]** and Ionn **[59]**. However, much the most important contributions to the mapping of the city are two large scale plans, those of Millard and Manning in 1830 **[53]**, and of Manning alone in c.1834 **[55]**. Together these fine productions provide the essential basis for a study of the city at the period when rapid expansion beyond the line of the walls was already under way, but the railway era had not yet begun.

Finally mention needs to be made of the prospects and the panoramas. As the true survey gained acceptance, the panoramic view received a new lease of life through the superbly produced North-East Prospect of Kirkpatrick **[22]**, and the smaller and better known North-East and South-East Prospects of Samuel and Nathaniel Buck **[31]** and **[32]**. The 18th century saw a number of smaller derivatives, and copies of the Buck Prospects were still being produced in the 19th century. Those prints which were clearly copied from Kirkpatrick or the Bucks which have been identified have been included in the list. The 18th century also saw the production of an increasing number of prints of all kinds depicting the buildings and life of the city, which have not been included as they are outside the scope of this work.

1. Described in the later text on the reverse of Braun & Hogenberg's plan **[2]** as ' Norvvicus....amplissima Angliae urbs Londino non immerito comparanda...' A similar brief description appears in the Index which is included in some editions of the third volume of the *Civitates Orbis Terrarum*.
2. The only other known contemporary printed map of an English town, of which no complete copy of the engraving has been found, is the so-called 'lost copperplate' map of London; dated between 1553 and 1559 (with an inclination towards the latter), of which only three out of a possible twelve or fifteen plates have been discovered. See Delano-Smith and Kain, *English Maps: A History*, p.190 and notes.
3. It was reluctantly decided not to attempt to include manuscript plans, which would include the Sanctuary Map of 1541, referred to in Cuningham **[1]**, note 4, through to the tithe maps of the early 19th century. The comparatively small number which are known are to be found in the BL, the PRO, the NRO, and the Castle, and deserve a separate study.
4. The Ordnance Survey drafted but did not publish a separate plan of the city of Norwich, but it has been included partly because the Norwich section formed the basis of the plans of Dawson **[54]**, **[60]** and **[61]** and of Creighton **[58]** which are listed, and partly because of its significance for all subsequent mapping.
5. Stephen includes on p.216 the etching by Thomas Rowlandson of 1799, with an illustration, (BL Maps K.Top.31.34.(d.)). This seems to be more correctly described as an artistic view. With the example of the print in the British Library, is another view by Rowlandson, of Great Yarmouth Market Place, in a very similar style, (BL Maps K.Top.31.40.c).
6. See James Elliot *The City in Maps* London, 1987; significant articles in *The Cartographic Journal* by David Smith, vol. 28, December 1991, p.163, and vol. 29, December 1992, p.118; and Delano-Smith and Kain *English Maps: A History*, the chapter on *Mapping Towns*, with references in extensive notes.
7. Darlington and Howgego, *Maps of London*.
8. For a discussion of the boundaries see the notes by John Kirkpatrick in *The Streets and Lanes*, and an article by W.C.Ewing in *Norfolk Archaeology*, vol.II, p.1, 1847, with a plan of the city showing the boundaries at the time of Philip and Mary.
9. Hudson and Tingey *Records* Vol. I, with plan opposite p.46.
10. Although the outer boundaries were not shown on many of the city plans, the boundaries were shown on large scale maps of the county, e.g. Faden in 1797, (Chubb p.78), and Bryant in 1826, (Chubb p.106), and on G. & J. Cary's *Improved Map of England and Wales* in 1832.

Plate 1 [2] 1581 Georg Braun and Franz Hogenburg

Plate 2 [13] c.1666 (1676) John Speed

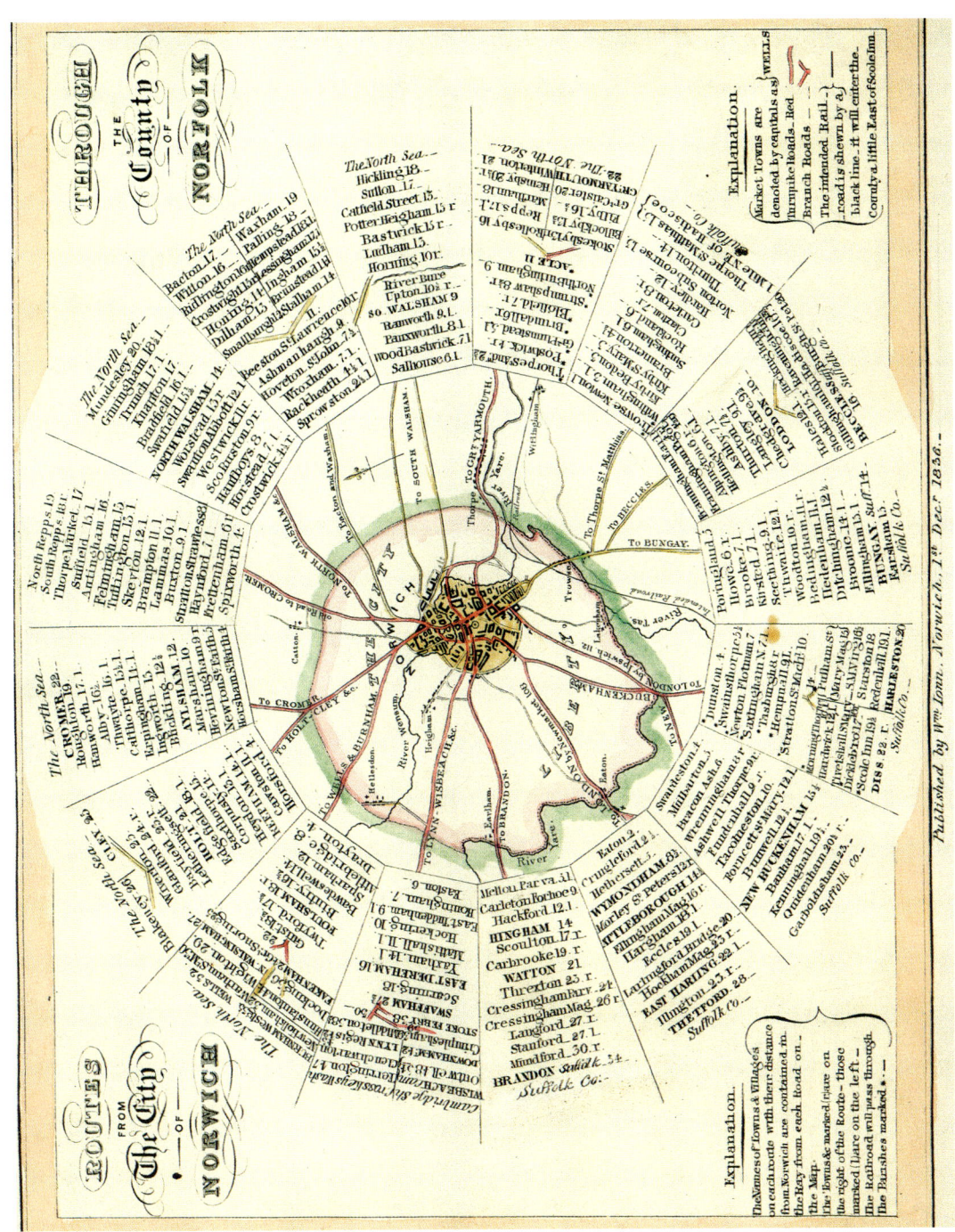

Plate 3 [59] 1836 William Ionn

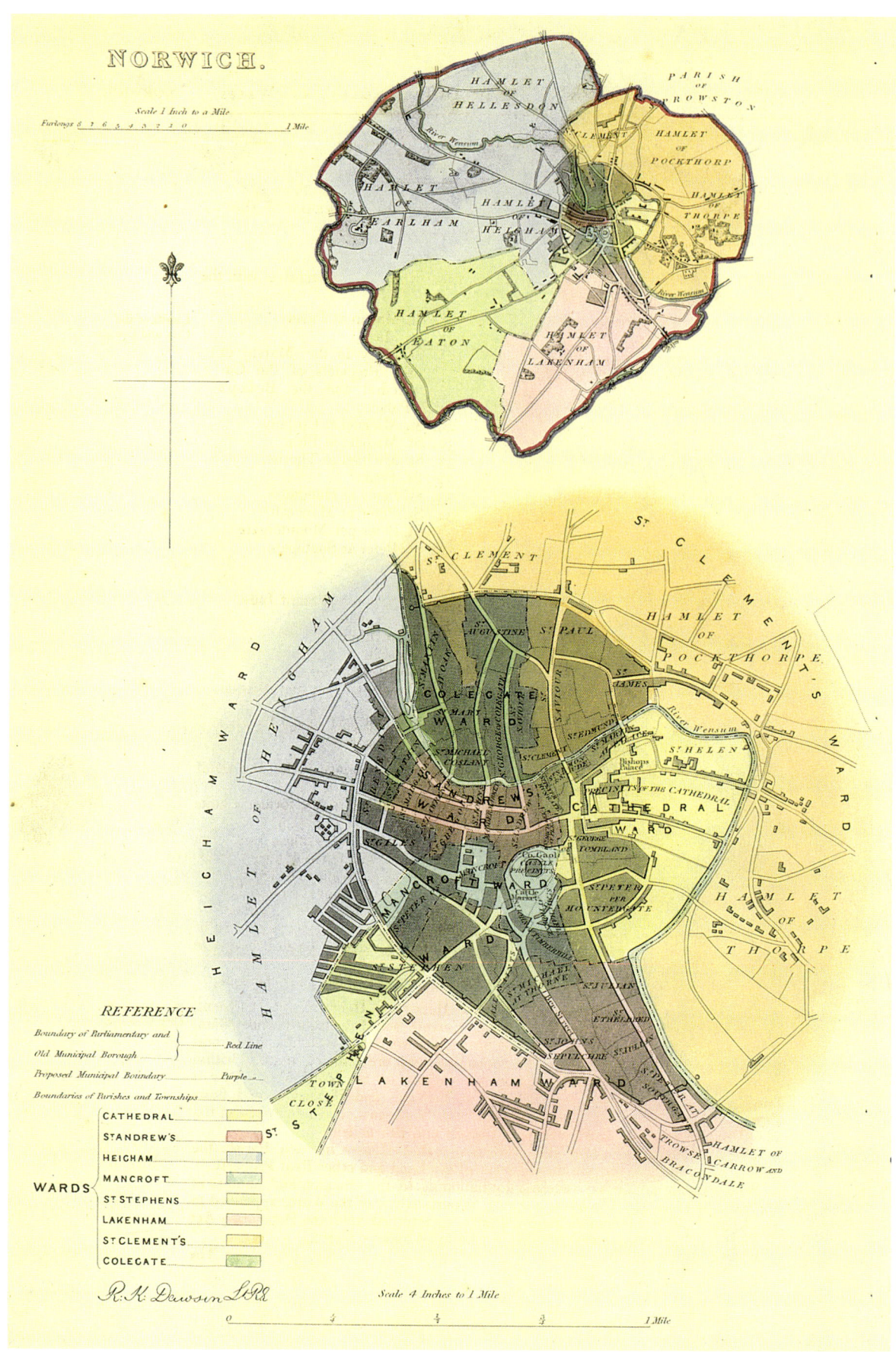

Plate 4 [60 & 61] 1837 Robert K. Dawson

[1] WILLIAM CUNINGHAM   London   1558

NORDOVICUM, ANGLIAE CIVITAS   ANNO • 1558 •   I.B•F[1]   300 x 405 mm.

Source
From *The Cosmographical Glasse, conteinyng the pleasant Principles of Cosmographie, Geographie, Hydrographie, or Nauigation. Compiled by VVilliam Cuningham Doctor in Physicke.*[2] *Excussum Londini in officina Ioan Daij Typographi.*[3] *Anno 1559*. The book was *Imprinted at London by John Day, dwelling over Aldersgate, beneath St. Martin's. 1559.* The plan of Norwich is placed before folio 9 in the book. The first printing of the book contains the plan in State 1; later printings do not show any changes in the date or the text, but contain the plan in State 2.

Origin of the Plan
This is the earliest surviving printed map of any English town. It is also the first authentic plan of the city, and it has no known antecedents. The only known earlier plan of the city as a whole is the manuscript Sanctuary Map of 1541.[4] There is every reason to believe that the plan was drawn by William Cuningham himself. He was in Norwich from 1556 to 1559, and he says (folio 8 of the book) that he has shown the city as it was in 'this present 1558'. The Preface to the book is signed by Cuningham at Norwich, 18th July 1559.

It is possible that some of the many wood-cuts in the book may have been engraved by Cuningham personally, but it is unlikely that he was the engraver of the plan. The name of the engraver has not been positively identified, but it is thought that this was John Bettes, whose initials I.B. (I.B.fecit) are in the title scroll. The same initials, I.B.•F, also appear on the title page of the book, and in at least one of the initial letters.[5] Little note however seems to be have been taken of the monogram 'J/F', which appears to be a signature in the bottom right corner of the plan in State 1, and as the signature of the portrait of Cuningham, again in State 1, in the front of the book. However the monogram is missing from the second states of both the plan and the portrait, and must have been deliberately removed. The plan, the title page, and the portrait are the three most important illustrations in the work, and the full extent of Bettes' responsibility, and the identity of 'J/F' must remain matters for conjecture.

Description (State 1)
A wood engraving, being a panoramic view of the city, as it might be seen by an observer looking down on the city from the west. Within the city walls the pattern of the roads can be clearly followed, with the exception of part of King Street hidden beneath the hillside beyond Ber Street. In the foreground, within the walls, there are cattle grazing in Chapelfield; the market cross is just visible in the market place; the castle and cathedral are prominently shown; the overall impression is of tightly packed houses in the centre of the city, of the numerous churches, but also much open space, particularly in the northern part of the city and along the river. Boats are shown on the river upstream of the New Mills. Apart from a few isolated properties,[6] the only developments outside the walls are the small suburbs of Pockthorpe and Heigham. Otherwise there are open fields, with Eaton Wood bottom right,[7] two windmills on Mousehold Heath (a feature of most subsequent city plans derived from Cuningham), Thorpe Wood across the river from Bishop Bridge, and the river disappearing downstream into the distance beyond Thorpe village towards Great Yarmouth.[8]

Above the city in a pattern of clouds are, top left, the royal arms between two cherubs, top right, the city arms likewise held by two cherubs, and, in the centre, Mercury above a scroll containing the title. In the foreground, outside the walls, stand two figures, presumably Cuningham and his

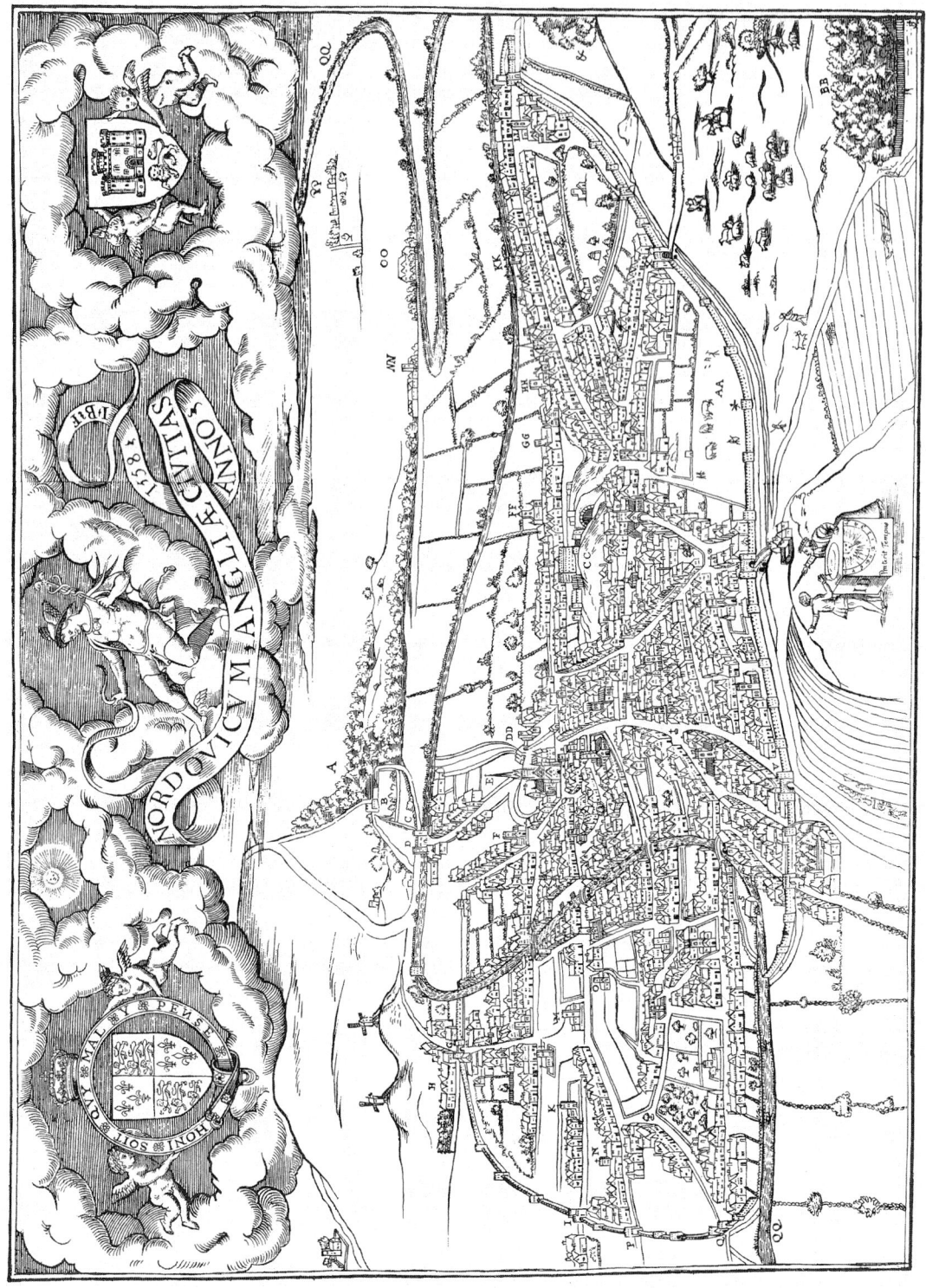

[1] 1558 William Cuningham

assistant with their surveying equipment, the assistant with compasses, and both pointing over the city towards the north. They stand either side of a table, (perhaps the 'Geographicall plaine sphere' described in the text); on the front are the words 'Preterit Tempus' beneath a sundial; on the left are the initials of John Day, 'I D'. In the extreme bottom right corner of the plan beneath Eaton Wood is the monogram 'J/ F'.

On the back of the plan is the key containing references to features on the plan itself, with the direction that 'This picture must be placed before the 9 leafe'.[9]

Description (State 2)

The plan in State 2 contains a number of minor amendments. The engraving of the sundial has been strengthened, and the top of the table has been re-engraved as a compass indicator. Additional figures, who appear to be archers target practising, have appeared in Chapelfield, together with one extra cow. The letters 'II' shown in the key as 'S. Michaels' have been added. Finally, in the bottom right corner the border lines have been re-engraved as has part of Eaton Wood, and the monogram 'J/F' has been removed.

Later History

John Day was granted a royal licence to print Cuningham's work, and surviving copies indicate several printings, although the only changes noted are those to the plan, and the portrait, already mentioned. There is no evidence that Day sold copies of the plan in its first two states separately from the book. However the plan was later issued in a third state with another publication. Queen Elizabeth visited Norwich in 1578, in the course of a royal progress. The visit was described in a number of contemporary publications,[10] including *Queen Elizabeth's Progress to Norwich, A° 1578, collected by B.G. and T.C. imprinted at London by Henry Bynneman, with a map of Norwich city, by John Day.*[11] Although firm evidence is lacking, it may be that at the time of this publication copies of the plan were sold separately.

For reproductions of the plan see, (inter alia), Richard Taylor's *Nordovicum* [53], the issue of *The Graphic* for 25 August 1883, and Kirkpatrick, *Street and Lanes*.

Description (State 3)

No further changes have been made to the actual plan of the city, but the date *ANNO 1558* has been deleted from the title. There is a new outer border of one outer and two inner lines. What was originally the bottom border of the plan in State 2 has been replaced by a new border above the line of the original, thus slightly reducing the depth of the plan. The key or table of references originally printed on the back on the plan has now been added, without any correction or alteration, below the bottom border, together with the words in the bottom right corner *Imprinted at London by John Daye.*

1. Stephen p.193 (1558), with illustration (State 2).; BL 59.i.28 (State 2); Bod Douce C Subt.112 (State 2); CUL bb.77.55.1 (State 2); Nfk.Lib. (State 1); Castle (State 3). *The Cosmographical Glasse* has been reprinted, (with plan in State 2), in the series of Early Printed Books published in facsimile, by Theatrum Orbis Terrarum, Amsterdam and New York, 1968.
2. William Cuningham, b. 1531, d. post 1586, probably a native of Norfolk, studied at Corpus Christi College, Cambridge, and at Heidelberg. He was practising as a physician in Norwich 1556-1559, and after leaving Norwich became eminent in London as a physician, and also as mathematician, cosmographer, and astronomer. References to Cuningham are found in many books on map making: see Delano-Smith and Kain, *English Maps*, p.185 ff.; D.N.B; Blomefield, *Norwich*, Vol.I, p.278; E.G.R.Taylor, *Mathematical Practitioners of Tudor England 1485-1714*, Cambridge, 1970.
3. John Day, printer and publisher, 1522-1584. Day was a reformer, and had spent some time in prison during the reign of Mary. Following the accession of Elizabeth in 1558 he became a leading London printer, his work including the first English edition of Foxe's Book of Martyrs.

4. Produced pursuant to the Statute 32 Henry VIII c. 12 (PRO MPI 1/221), Stephen p. 191 (1541); illustrated in Kirkpatrick, *Streets and Lanes*; Harvey, *Maps in Tudor England*.

5. Apart from the initials on the plan itself there is no contemporary evidence of the identity of the engraver, but the name of Bettes appears in later publications: from Granger's *Biographical History of England*, 'Cuningham executed several cuts himself. The map is by a different hand. This is by John Bettes.'; Gough in *British Topography* refers to John Bettes as the likely engraver; from A.M.Hind, *Engraving in England*, Cambridge, 1952, 'John Bettes, woodcutter and engraver, very probable he was cutter of the table and border with Mercury.'

6. Outside the city gates were five leper hospitals. The plan shows these outside Magdalen Gates, and in the foreground outside St. Giles Gate. The hospitals were still in use during the 16th century for receiving sufferers of contagious diseases; see Carole Rawcliffe, *The Hospitals of Mediaeval Norwich*, Norwich, 1995. They are clearly shown on Kirkpatrick's plan [23].

7. Eaton Wood is shown as a prominent feature in the bottom corner of the plan; in 1549 Kett and his rebels arrived there on their way from Wymondham. Having been refused permission to pass through the city they stayed there overnight, before moving on to their permanent camp on Mousehold.

8. In the text of the book Cuningham includes a short description of the city : ' Norwiche an healthful & pleasant Citye, having a faire river called Yerus, ronning thorow it, which cometh out of the seas frõ Yermouthe coste. It is much subject to fiers, which have not little hindered the beauty thereof. The picture of it you will find lively set out in the first boke [the plan]: the longitude & latitude 22.30 and 52.10.'

9. Care must be taken in the use of the key and the plan in identifying particular buildings, and especially the numerous churches. Many of the churches (e.g. St. Peter Mancroft) are not identified by name, and there are discrepancies between the known position of certain churches which have subsequently been demolished, and their position shown on the plan. A detailed study of the plan is beyond the scope of these notes, but there are a number of discrepancies between the key and the plan, including among the more obvious: two letters, L and O, are shown on the plan but not on the key ; what is shown on the plan as 'The hospitall' (DD) is in fact the then existing church in the Close of St. Mary in the Marsh; the hospital, St. Helen's in Bishopgate, has no key letter; II on the key is not shown on the first state of the plan, but was added to the second; the letters KK and OO are on the plan but not on the key.

10. An extensive account of the visit is included in Holinshed's *Chronicles*, in the augmented *Chronicles* after the year 1577 (BL 629.n.3.). The marginal note on fo.1287 indicates a contemporary report by 'B.G.' and 'T.G.', the authors of the work referred to in the text. A further account is found in *The ioyfull receyuing of the Queeenes most excellent Majestie into hir Highnesse Citie of Norwich.....*published by Henry Bynnemam, 1578 (BL C.33.d.2.), which however does not contain the plan. In respect of the work containing the plan Blomefield, *Norwich*, Vol.II, p. 317, refers to Stow's Supplement to Holinshed, and it is also mentioned by Gough in *British Topography*, but no original copy of the work has been found.

[2] GEORG BRAUN and FRANZ HOGENBERG   Cologne   1581

NORDOVICUM, ANGLIAE CIVITAS[1]   295 x 300 mm.

Source

From *Urbium Praecipuarum Totius Mundi - Liber Tertius*, being the Third Book of the six volume work known as *Civitates Orbis Terrarum* published in Cologne in 1581. The text of Book Three was printed by Gottfried von Kempen. Planned and produced by Georg Braun[2] and Franz Hogenberg,[3] the *Civitates* was published between 1572 and 1618. With its 363 plans or prospects of mainly European cities, it is one Europe's great cartographic works.

Origin of the plan

The plan of Norwich was engraved by Franz Hogenberg, and close examination shows that it is an almost exact copy of the second state of the plan of William Cuningham [1]. For certain English cities Braun made use of the work of William Smith, whose manuscript plan of Norwich would have been known to him;[4] however it is likely that Braun would have been familiar with the *Cosmographical Glasse*, and he was clearly able to obtain a copy of Cuningham's plan.

There is no signature or imprint, but the surrounding decoration and details have been identified as the work of Joris Hoefnagel.[5]

Description (State 1)

A plan or prospect of the city as viewed from the west, being a very close copy of the plan of Cuningham [1]. The boats on the river are missing. Differences are in the title, the coats of arms, the references, and in particular the figures in the foreground. The title is in an ornamental panel top centre, the royal arms top left, the city arms in a wreath top right, references in a panel bottom left, and a man and a woman in contemporary Elizabethan costume bottom centre. A considerable number of editions of the *Civitates* were produced, with the text in Latin, French and German; in each edition the plan is unchanged, but there are a number of different settings of the text. A number of editions were issued undated, and it is not always easy positively to relate different settings to a particular date of publication.[6]

The Text

Each of the plans has, on its reverse, information about the town or city illustrated. The Norwich description is of particular interest, as in addition to routine details about the City, the text concludes with a poem. This is stated to have been written by the poet Daniel Rogers, and that it had been delivered before the Queen 'and a number of ambassadors' during a visit to Norwich. This was clearly the well documented week's visit of Queen Elizabeth to the city in 1578, during which many orations and loyal addresses were made, and it is known that three French ambassadors were present with the Queen.[7] The translation provided by Stephen is worthy of repeating; its contemporary setting is shown by the reference to 'Belgic friends', who are the 'Strangers' recently arrived from the Netherlands, while it was generally considered at the time that Norwich was the Venta Icenorum of the Romans:

> Norwich may rightly pay respect to London's prior claim;
> And offer reverence to York of venerable fame;
> But doubt if justice bids her yield to Bristol all the same.
> Just weigh their assets: Each of them a Bishop's state enstalls;
> And each is castle-guarded, and begirt with lofty wall.
> Far-famed for commerce each of them; their trade beyond compare;
> The one by way of Severn's streams, the other of the Yare.
> The land round each is fertile; and each city richly glows
> Adorned in cultured opulence which civic zeal bestows.
> In population Norwich leads, and in her ample space;
> For ships that traverse every ocean Bristol is the place.
> To Belgic friends both these and those have kind alliance shown,
> Whence equal praise and profit have alike to either grown.
> What both could do they gave good cause for Danish hosts to know;
> And both have well sustained the weight of Norman's mighty blow.
> Rank equal then, ye cities twin, and bear in mind this truth-
> The name of each was Venta once - one name the same for both:
> For Venta of the Belgics was the Bristol town of yore,
> And Venta Icenorum was the name that Norwich bore.

Later History

In 1653, after the deaths of both Georg Braun and Franz Hogenberg, the plates of the *Civitates* (including that of Norwich) were sold by Abraham Hogenberg to Joannes Jassonius (Jan Jansson). Janssonius decided to reissue these with alterations in a series of eight Townbooks. Following the death of Janssonius in 1664 the plates passed to his son in law Joannes Jansson van

Waesberge, who died in 1681. Shortly following the death of van Waesberge 236 of the Braun and Hogenberg plates, as now altered, including the plate of Norwich, were published in two volumes. Although many of the plates were subsequently acquired by Frederick de Wit and published by him in his Townbooks, they did not include Norwich.

The Norwich plan is therefore found, in **State 2,** in the following publications -

a. In Part VI of the Townbooks of Janssonius, with the title *Theatrum Praecipuarum Europae Plagam - Illustriorum Principumque Urbium Septentrionalium Europae Tabulae Amstelodami Ex officina Joannis Jansonnii*, published in **Amsterdam** in **1657**; the Norwich plan has Latin text on the back, reset, but not corrected from the 'Nevers' version in the final edition of Braun and Hogenberg. The verses are in a single column.[8]

b. In *Tooneel der Vermaste Koop Steden en Handel-plaatsen van de geheele Werwld - Tweede Deel*, (Number 29 out of 111), published by van Waesberge's heirs in **Amsterdam** in **1682**. There is no accompanying text.

Description (State 2)

The title has been changed to **NORDOVICUM**, in a revised surrounding scroll. However the most obvious difference from State 1 of the plan is the deletion of the two figures in the foreground, whose dress might have looked out of place in the latter half of the seventeenth century. The panel containing the references has been re-engraved, but the actual plan of the city has not ben changed.

1. Stephen p.195 (1580-83), p. 198 (1616). BL 215.f.3 ; BL Add. MS 23037.f.33; Bod Gough Norfolk Maps 1; Nfk.Lib.; Castle; RCF.
2. Georg Braun, 1541-1590, a native of Cologne and distinguished cleric; he liaised with many others, both on the continent and elsewhere, to obtain drafts of plans, and information for the accompanying text of his work. These included Abraham Ortelius, whose *Theatrum Orbis Terrarum* provded an inspiration for the *Civitatis*.
3. Franz Hogenberg ,1535-1590, a protestant engraver born in Mechelen, and a contributor as an engraver to the *Theatrum Orbis Terrarum* of Ortelius.
4. See Speed [4], note 3.
5. Joris Hoefnagel, 1542-1610, son of an Antwerp artist, painter and topographer, working in England 1568-69, who drafted and whose signature is found on many of the plans in the *Civitatis*.
6. See the Introduction by R.A.Skelton to the facsimile reprint of the *Civitatis* by Theatrum Orbis Terrarum, 1965. Editions of the Norwich plan include the following -

a. **Latin** editions were issued in 1581, 1588, 1593, 1599, 1606, 1612, 1616.

There are various settings of the text; in most the verses are printed in two columns, and with one exception, no significant variations in the actual content have been noted. Variations in the settings include the following -

    i. Heading NORVVICUS. (100mm) ; first line ends '...ciuitas &'; last line - 'exciperetur'.

    ii. Heading as above (80mm) ; first line ends '..ciuitas'; last line as above

    iii. Heading as above (75mm) ; first line ends '...ciuitas'; last line - 'gnifico istic apparatu, varijs comitatae Legatis'.

    iv. Heading as above (80mm); first line ends '...inter'; last line -' tata legatis, exciperetur'.

    v. Heading as above (100mm) ; first line ends '....& una inter'; last line -' co, cum......varijs comitatatu legatis, exciperetur'.

    vi. Heading as above (95mm), with smaller print and the only edition with the poem printed in one column. This appears to have been the last Latin edition to have ben published, and has a peculiarity in that there is an additional introductory paragraph, and very curiously there is included at the beginning of the next paragraph a section which properly relates not to Norwich but to Novidunum (Nevers) in France. The section does also appear correctly in its proper place on the reverse of the plan of Nevers (number 10, also in Book Three).

b. A **German** edition was issued in 1582, and at least one other is recorded. Although the German text refers to Daniel Rogers and his poem, the poem itself is not included.

c. **French** editions were issued in 1583, and later . The poem is included (still in Latin), printed in two columns. Different settings of the text, seven in the Bibliothèque Nationale, include the following -

    i. Heading NORTVVICH. (100mm) ; third line ends 'Oriental:'.

ii. Heading as above (95mm) ; third line ends 'laquelle les'.
7. See Cuningham [1] note 10.
8. BL Maps C.25.b.10.

Illustration Plate 1

[3] FRANCISCO VALEZO   Venice   1595

NORDOVICUM. ANGLIAE CIVITAS[1]   90 x 130 mm.

Source
From *Raccolta di le piu illustri et famose citta di tutto il mondo*, published in Venice in 1595. This small volume contains 255 plates engraved by Valezo[2] and others, without text. The backs are plain. In addition to Norwich, the work contains plans of Bristol, Cambridge, Canterbury, Chester, London and Edinburgh.

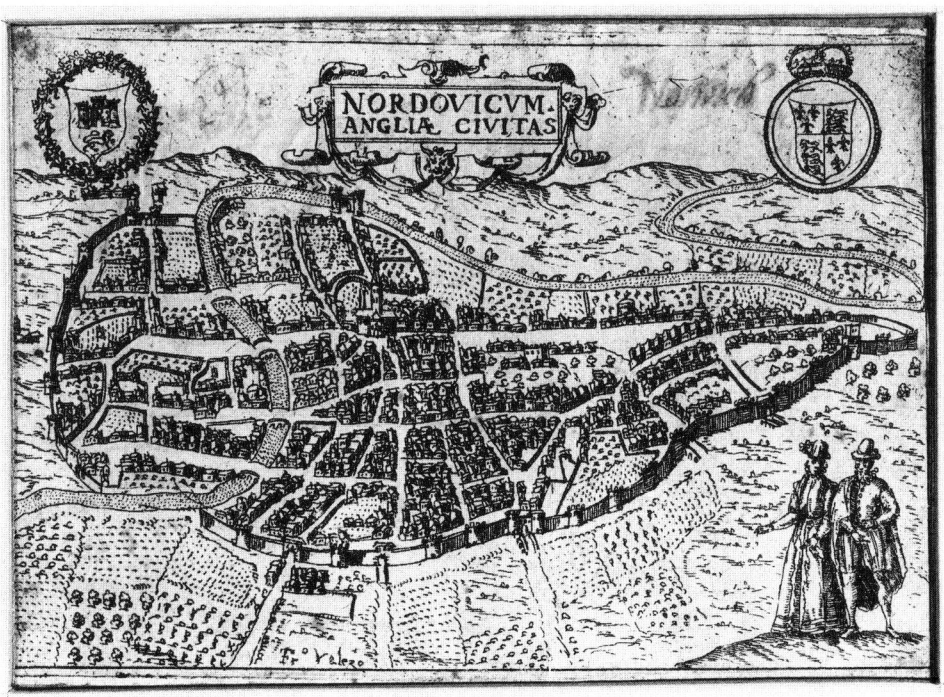

[3] 1595 Francisco Valezo

Description
A small perspective plan of the city, clearly based on Braun and Hogenberg [2]. The reduced size means less detail, but the river and the city walls are clearly shown, as is the pattern of roads within the walls. The title, top centre, is in an ornamental panel. Two figures, bottom right, are copied from Braun and Hogenberg, but face left and not right. The city arms, top left, are reversed, as are the royal arms, top right. The name of the engraver *Fr° Valezo* is close to the bottom border, which is formed by a thin line.

Later History
The Norwich plan is found in the following publications -

a. A further edition of the work, entitled as above, with 330 plates, but without alteration to the plan, was published in **Venice** in **1595**.

b. A further edition, now entitled *Teatro delle piu illustri et famose citta del mondo*, was published in **Venice** by Donato Rasciotti in **1600**. This work, which is without text, contains 78 pages with two plans on each page; Norwich is below the plan of London, and on the facing page are plans of Bristol and Edinburgh. The backs are plain.[3]

c. The plan was republished without alteration by Alphonsus Lasor a Varea, (a pseudonym of Raphael Savanarola) in *Universus terrarum orbis scriptorum calamo delineatus... qui de Europae, Asiae, Africae & Americae. Patavii ex typographia olim Frambotti, nunc J.B.Conzatti*, in **Padua** in **1713**.[4] This work consists of two folio volumes, containing numerous maps and plans, which are incorporated in the text. The Norwich plan (a rather weak impression) is found towards the top of page 263 in Volume 2, with a few lines of text, in Latin, about Norwich - that it is the capital of Norfolk, a bishopric within the archbishopric of Canterbury, on the River Yare, and that it is 16 miles from the German Ocean at Yarmouth, 32 miles from Lynn and Ipswich, and 95 from London. The page also contains a separate short section about Norfolk, but there is no map of the county. On the reverse, page 264, is a continuation of the text, with a plan of Nuremberg.

1. Stephen p. 197 (1595). BL Maps c.24.a.5; Nfk.Lib.
2. Francisco Valezo, otherwise known as Valeso, or Valegio, a painter and engraver born in Bologna c.1560.
3. BL Maps c.25.a.10
4. BL 128.g.13

[4] JOHN SPEED (Plate 1)   London   1610

NORWICHE[1]   95 x 175 mm.

Source

The bird's-eye plan of Norwich is in the top right corner of the map of the county of Norfolk (375 x 505 mm.), known in proof form, but first published in *The Theatre of The Empire of Great Britaine......Described by John Speed. Imprinted at London. Anno 1611*. Although the Norfolk map is undated, the maps of many other counties (e.g. Suffolk, Essex, Cambridgeshire) are dated 1610, and Norfolk is likely to have been completed at least in proof form on or before that date. Many of the county maps, although not that of Norfolk, bear the signature of Jodocus Hondius,[2] and all are thought to have been engraved by him or under his direction in Amsterdam; a later edition of the Norfolk plate is signed *R. Elstrack Sculpsit*, but it is uncertain as to whether he engraved the original plate, or, more likely, that he was only responsible for subsequent alterations.

Origin of the Plan

Speed would almost certainly have known of Cuningham's plan in *The Cosmographical Glasse* [1], and would also have been familiar with the *Civitates* of Braun and Hogenberg [2]. A number of his town plans in the *Theatre* were based on plans in the *Civitates*. However close inspection indicates that Speed's plan was based directly on neither Cuningham nor Braun and Hogenberg, but on a manuscript plan of William Smith. This was not the result of a new survey, but was itself copied from Cuningham. It was included with manuscript plans of a number of other English cities in *The Particular Description of England*, which was dated 1588, but which in the event was not published until the 19th century.[3]

Description

The plan is a panoramic view of Norwich, similar in aspect to those of Cuningham and of Braun and Hogenberg, but it is very much smaller, and consequently has less detail. Nevertheless the plan is neatly engraved, the road pattern is clearly shown within the city walls, the river extends downstream towards and beyond Thorpe, and the two windmills on Mousehold are prominently featured. Boats are shown upstream of the New Mills (as with Cuningham and William Smith, but not with Braun and Hogenberg). A feature of William Smith's plan, which was coloured, is that part of the ditch along the western side of the city wall has been shown as a moat. With the possible exception of a short stretch of wall between Heigham Gate (Hell Gate) and the river, the ditch outside the walls was never water filled, but the error was repeated in a number of later plans. The Speed plan clearly shows the ditch, although it is not immediately apparent from the drawing whether it is dry or water filled; as a result copies of the plan are often wrongly coloured. The title is in a decorated panel top centre, against the top margin of the map; in the top left corner are 'The Armes of Norwiche' with letters indicating the heraldic colours; there is an outline compass indicator bottom right; below the plan is a panel (40 x 67 mm.) containing 'PLACES within the Cittie obserued by letters'. The border of plan and panel is formed by two thin lines.

Later History

A number of alterations were made to the plate of the map in subsequent years, but no changes were made to the plan of Norwich. Including a proof, at least seven states of the plate of the map are known; successive editions saw the addition of shading to the sea, and of Roman names, the battle scene in the top left corner was replaced, and eventually cracking appeared which resulted in the plate being scrapped. The last edition of the *Theatre* in which this plate was used was published in **c.1665**; the Norfolk map has the imprint of *Roger Rea ye Elder and younger at ye Golden Crosse in Cornhill against the Exchange*. Following the scrapping of the original plate, a new plate was engraved in c.1666 by John Goddard and was used for all later editions of the *Theatre* [13].

1. Stephen p.198 (1611, 1627), and the county maps of Norfolk referred to by Chubb, which entries are in need of revision. Many examples, including BL Maps C.7.c.5.(35.); Bod Gough Maps 92; Nfk.Lib.; Castle; RCF.
2. Jodocus Hondius senior, 1563-1612, engraver and publisher, left Ghent for London as a refugee for London in 1583, returning to the Netherlands ten years later.
3. William Smith, c.1550 -1618, herald and topographer. His plan is included in Stephen under the year 1588, the date of *The Particular Description,* but it was almost certainly drawn some years earlier. The publication of the work in 1879 included a lithographic copy of the Norwich plan. The original is in the BL, Sloane MS. 2596,*f.*61; illustrated in colour in Harvey, *Maps in Tudor England.* William Smith planned a series of county maps, also engraved by Jodocus Hondius, of which only twelve (including that of Norfolk) were eventually published, (Chubb p.3, 1602, in need of revision).

[5]   JODOCUS HONDIUS (JUNIOR) (1)   **Amsterdam**   **1617**

Norwiche[1]   30 x 60 mm.

Source

Norwich is one of a number of small town plans within the top and bottom borders of a map of the British Isles (380 x 510 mm.), a separate publication entitled *Magnae Britanniae et Hiberniae*

Tabula, with the imprint *Amstelodami Ex Officina et sumptibus Jodoci Hondii A° Domini 1617.*[2] The plan of Norwich is within the bottom border, between Edinburgh and Dublin. The other towns represented are Hereford, Oxford, York, London, Canterbury, Cambridge, Newcastle, Galway, Bristol, Chester and Coventry.[2]

Origin of the Plan
The plan is a much reduced version of that of Speed [4].[3] Border scenes became a common and attractive feature of maps, particularly by the Dutch cartographers of the 17th century.[4] Known as *cartes à figures*, many of these contain miniature town plans, although examples which contain British towns are rare. Norwich plans are found on maps published in the Netherlands by Visscher [6], another by Jodocus Hondius Junior [7], and by Verbiest [8]. Later British examples are those by Stent [11] and Walton [14].

Description
The city is readily identifiable by the outline of the city walls, the two windmills top left, and the river running away into the distance top right. The engraving is clear, as one would expect from the engraver, and one can pick out the street pattern, but the size is such that, apart from the cathedral, it is difficult to identify individual buildings. The title is top centre.

Later History
The map is the original version of the map of the British Isles which appears in the Mercator-Hondius *Atlas* of 1633, with the signature of Henricus Hondius, and dated 1631.[5] However by this time the decorated borders, including the town plans, have been removed.

1. Not in Stephen. Shirley, *British Isles*, 1970, no. 355a, p.131.3. Only one example of the map with the decorated borders has been found. The map is illustrated in Shirley, Plate 110, p. 132, and the same map is illustrated in *The Map Collector* No.32, September 1985, p.36. The British Library has a copy of the map in its first state, but it has been trimmed and the borders have been removed, BL Maps 185.m.2.(6.).
2. Jodocus Hondius junior, 1594-1624, Amsterdam printer, engraver, cartographer and publisher. He was the elder son of Jodocus Hondius senior; see Speed [4], note 2.
3.. The maps in Speed's *Theatre of the Empire of Great Britain* [4], had been engraved by, or under the direction of, Jodocus Hondius senior; the Norwich plan by Jodocus Hondius junior appears to have been based on Speed, rather than directly on Braun and Hogenberg [2] or Cuningham [1].
4. *Jodocus Hondius, Creator of the Decorative Map Border*, by Günter Schilder, *The Map Collector* No.32, September 1985, pp. 40-43.
5. Henricus Hondius, 1597-1651, brother of Jodocus Hondius junior, and younger son of Jodocus Hondius senior.

[6]   CLAES JANSZOON VISSCHER   Amsterdam   c.1623

NORWICHE[1]   40 x 65 mm.

Source
From a map of Great Britain (465 x 550 mm.), a separate publication entitled *Tabulae Magnae Britanniae continens Angliam Scotiam et Hiberniam nuperimè edita per Nicolaum Iohannis Visscher*, with imprints *Impressa in aedibus Nicolaij Johannis Visscher,*[2] and *Abraham Goos sculp.*[3] (State 1 of the plate).[4]

Description
A tiny plan of the city, one of twelve bird's-eye town plans in the upper and lower borders of the

map of Great Britain. Along the top border are Newcastle, Cambridge, London, Edinburgh, Canterbury and York, and along the bottom border, Oxford, Galway, Dublin, Norwich, Bristol and Chester. The plan is similar to that of Jodocus Hondius Junior [5]. The map follows the map of the British Isles by Speed in outline and topographical details, and the Norwich plan is again based either directly on Speed [4], or on the 1617 plan of Jodocus Hondius Junior [5]. However the engraving is firm, the detail is clearer, and the road patterns more distinct. The ditch outside the city wall in the foreground is incorrectly shown as a branch of the river.[5] The title is in the surrounding border above the plan, and the plan itself is at a somewhat higher level within its section of the border; the result is to increase the amount of foreground outside the city wall, and to make the windmills and the river at the top of the plan much less prominent features.

Later History

The plan of Norwich was not altered, but the map was reissued -

a. Again as a separate publication, including the town plans, in **Amsterdam** in **1630**. The only alteration to the plate is the addition of the date 1630 after the imprint of Abraham Goos. (State 2 of the plate).

b. The map was again reissued, with the town plans, in **Amsterdam** in **1650**, by Nicolaus Visscher, the son of C.J.Visscher, probably as a separate publication. The map and plan are unchanged, save for the imprint, which is now *Tabula Magna Britannia continens Angliam Scotiam et Hiberniam nuperrime edita per Nicolaum Ioannis Visscher*, and the date 1650 is added over the engraver's signature. (State 3 of the plate).

c. The plate was subsequently reworked by Nicolaus Visscher, to produce what appears to be a new map with different decorative features, without the town plans.

1. Not in Stephen. BL Maps C.3.c.9, (the map in state 1, included as an additional map in a copy of the Mercator *Atlas* published by Henricus Hondius in Amsterdam in 1623).
2. Claes Janszoon Visscher, 1587-1652, engraver and publisher and founder of the Visschers' family business in the Kalverstraat in Amsterdam.
3. Abraham Goos, c.1590-1643, engraver, mapseller and publisher in Amsterdam.
4. For details of these maps, all of which are very rare, see Shirley, *British Isles,* 1970, number 384, with illustration, (Plate 114) p.138; number 421a, (state 2), and number 670, (state 3).
5. See the reference to the ditch outside the city wall in Speed [4]; in Visscher's plan the moat appears to extend along the wall from the river, which would have been physically impossible.

[7] JODOCUS HONDIUS (JUNIOR) (2)   **Amsterdam**   **c.1625**

NORWICHE[1]   40 x 60 mm.

Source

From a map of Great Britain (465 x 550 mm.), a separate publication entitled *Magnae Britanniae et Hiberniae Tabula*, with the imprint *Amstelodami Iodicus Hondius excudit* .(State 1 of the plate).[2]

Description

Another bird's-eye view of the city, in the lower border of the map of Great Britain. The map is a very close copy of the map of Visscher [6]. The plans are of the same towns in the same order, and the Norwich plan is an almost exact copy of Visscher's. There is a portrait of James I in the top left corner of the border of the map, indicating that the latest date for the plate is the year of his death, 1625; the portrait was however still retained in later editions of the map.[3]

Later History
a. The plate was acquired in 1629 from the heirs of Jodocus Hondius by Willem Janszoon Bleau.[3] In the absence of another plate of Great Britain being available, he decided to use it for his first world Atlas, the *Appendix Theatri A. Ortelii et Atlantis G. Mercatoris*, published in **Amsterdam** in **1630**. The map is unchanged, but the imprint now reads *Amstelodame Guiljelmus Blaeu excudit.* (State 2 of the plate).
b. The Atlas containing the map and the town plans was reissued in **1631**, and copies of the map were also available for a short time as separate sheets.
c. The border features, including the town plans, were then erased, and the map with the centre part extended formed the standard Blaeu map of the British Isles, first appearing in 1631. (State 3 of the plate).

1. Not in Stephen. Bibliothèque Nationale Ge. D. 8030. For further details and references see Shirley, *British Isles,* 1970, number 390, with illustration, (Plate 115), p.140; number 411, (state 2), and illustration (vi), p.xiii; and number 423, (state 3), and illustration, (Plate 128), p.152.
2. For Jodocus Hondius see [5] above, note 2.
3. William Janszoon Blaeu, 1571-1638, born in Alkmaar, established in Amsterdam business on his own account of instrument makers, cartographers, publishers and booksellers. Joined by his sons Joan, 1593-1673, and Cornelis, 1610-1648.

[8]   PIETER VERBIEST   **Antwerp**   **1629**

NORWICHE[1]   40 x 65 mm.

Source
One of a number of small town plans in the top and bottom border panels of a map of Great Britain (450 x 550 mm.), a separate publication entitled *Magnae Britanniae et Hiberniae Tabula,* with the imprint *Antwerpiensis Peterus ver Bistus A°.1629.* (State 1 of the plate).[2]

Description
Another tiny bird's-eye plan of the city. The map and plan are generally similar in style to those of Visscher [6]. The figures in the borders are different, and the town plans are now, along the top border, Newcastle, Cambridge, Norwich, London, Edinburgh and Canterbury, and along the bottom border, Oxford, Galway, Dublin, Montgomery, Bristol and Chester. The Norwich plan is sharply engraved, with the title above the border. There is more detail in the foreground than in most of the other similar small plans; the line of the city wall is prominent, with the ditch appearing to be part of the river, but because of the rounded ends of the panel the windmills have almost disappeared into the border, and most of the course of the river below the city has been lost.

Later History
The map was re-issued in **Antwerp** in **1646**, without any change to the plan. The only change to the plate is to the imprint, where the date has been corrected to *A°. 1646.* (State 2 of the plate).[3]

1. Not in Stephen. Shirley, *British Isles,* 1970, number 410, p.149.

2. Pieter Verbiest, otherwise Pieter or Petrus ver Bistus, 1605-1693, cartographer, engraver and publisher of Antwerp.
3. BL Maps 177.d.1.(11.); Shirley, *British Isles,* 1970, number 592, p. 197, with illustration, (Plate 155).

Illustration   Front Cover

[9] DANIEL MEISNER   **Frankfurt-am-Main**   **1631**

NORDOVICUM ANGL.[1]   100 x 145 mm.

Source
From a work which was published under the general title *Thesaurus Philo-Politicus,* between 1623 and 1631. It appeared as Books 1 and 2, each with 8 parts, and Norwich is plate 28 in Part 8 of Book 2, published in 1631. This has the title *Politischen Schatz-Kästleins .....Das ist Ausserlesene schöne Emblemata, oder Politische Moralia.....MDCXXXI.* The publisher was Eberhard Kieser in Frankfurt-am-Main. An introductory section contains a short explanation in German of the symbolism of the plans.[2]

[9] 1631 (1638) Daniel Meisner

Origin of the Plan
Daniel Meisner came from Comothau (Komothau) in Bohemia, was an author and poet, and was described as 'Poeta Laureatus Coronatus'. He was responsible for the planning of the work, but died in 1625, so did not live to see its complete publication. Nevertheless his name continued to

be associated with it throughout its publishing history. Each of the plans has a similar form to that of Norwich, with a picture, an inscription or motto, and two lines of verse below. They derive from a tradition of 'Emblemata' (Emblems) described in a number of 16th century publications; the sub title of *Thesaurus Philo-Politcus* is *Emblemata sive moralia politica*....and the source of the Norwich story is a work of Arnold Freitag *Mythologica Ethica, Hoc est Moralis philosophiae per fabulis brutis attributas traditae, amoenissimum viridarium*..... published in Antwerp in 1579.[3]

Description (State 1)

This very curious plan is based on that of Braun and Hogenberg [2], but it is a very sketchy version, barely recognisable except by the distinctive line of the city walls . The river is clearly shown passing through the city, but as with the plans of Visscher [6] and Verbiest [8], the ditch is incorrectly shown as a branch of the river along the outside of the wall. The only recognisable building within the walls is the cathedral. The city arms are shown top left, but reversed, with the lion facing right, (as on the plan of Valezo [3]). A large bay tree fills the right foreground, with a salamander on the ground beneath. The engraver's initials 'EL' are to the right of the tree, close to the border.[4]

The title is in a small central panel above the plan. Above the title along the top of the map are the words *REMEDIA AD SANITATEM CREATA SUNT* [Remedies were created to preserve health], with, top right, the plate number 28.

Beneath the plan is a further line of text *Inficitur corvus letalem ubi viciret hostem , At lauri folijs ipse venena necat,* [The raven when he has conquered his deadly enemy is poisoned, but he destroys the poison with the leaves of the bay tree].

Below the line in Latin are two lines in two columns in German -

Wann der raab ist vergifft davon   Vom Lorberbaum braucht Medicin
Dasser umbracht den Chameleon   Damit treibt er das gifft von ihm
[When the raven is poisoned because it killed the chameleon
It needs the medicine from the bay tree which expels the poison from him]

Description (State 2)

The plan in its second state appears in all editions after the first. The only change is the substitution of the plate number G49 for the original plate number 28.

Later History

a. The complete work, now under the title of *Sciographica Cosmica* was republished by Paulus Fürst in **Nuremberg**. In this edition Book 1 is dated 1637, and Book 2 **1638**; there are four parts in each Book, identified by the letters A to H. The British plans are all in Book 2, Part 7, with the plates identified by the letter G. Norwich is plate G49.

b. Further editions of *Sciographica Cosmica* were published by Paulus Fürst in **Nuremberg** in **1642** and **1678**, without changes to the plates.

c. An edition, again without change to the plates, but identifiable as being on larger paper was published with the title *Politica Politica* by Johann Helmers in **Nuremberg** in **1700**. A final edition was published by Johann Helmers in **Nuremberg** in **1704**, but only Book 1 of this date has been recorded.

---

1. Stephen p. 199 (1631), p. 200 (1638), p. 203 (1700), referred to as by 'E.L' (see note 4 below). BL Maps C. 26a. 31-38; Bod Douce S 162-3); Castle; Nfk.Lib.; RCF.
2. On page 15 of the Introduction, under the heading *28. Nordovicum in Engelland.* The text in translation reads - The chameleon which is a poisonous animal is killed by the raven. So the raven is poisoned by the animal and will have to die if it does not take any medicine. Therefore it eats the bay leaves (as its instinct tells it) and by these

means gets back its former health and strength.
3. The work, its various editions, and the background to its publication are fully described in the Introduction to a facsimile edition published in Nördlingen, Germany, in 1992.
4. EL are the initials of Johann Eckhard Löffler, an engraver working in Cologne from 1630 to 1678. 117 plates in the work carry his signature as EL, IEL, JEL, or L. The tree in the foreground is a typical feature of his work.

[10] RUTGERUS HERMANNIDES   Amsterdam   1661

NORDOVICUM . NORWICH.[1]   115 x 125 mm.

Source
From *Rutgeri Hermannide Britannia Magna, sive Angliae, Scotiae, Hiberniae et adjactentium Insularum geographico-historica descriptio. Amstelodami apud Aegidium Valckenier A°. 1661.* Pages 263-269 of the work, which is in Latin, are headed *Anglicanarum ad ortum Provinciarum - II NORTFOLCIA*. They contain a description of the county of Norfolk; the plan of Norwich, with no text on the back, is placed after page 264.

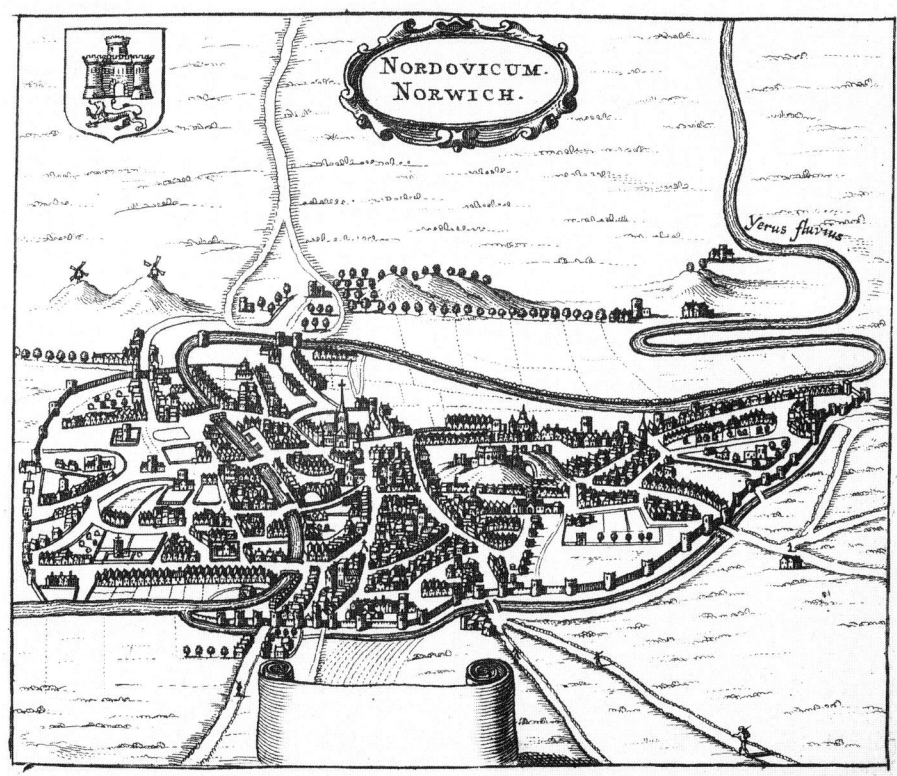

[10] 1661 Rutgerus Hermannides

Description
The plan is clearly engraved, and bears a striking resemblance to the plan of Speed [4] from which it was almost certainly taken. Particularly prominent features are the two windmills on Mousehold, and the river disappearing into the distance towards Yarmouth. The title, top centre, is in an oval cartouche; the city arms top left are correctly shown; at the bottom centre is a scroll which appears designed for some inscription, but in fact is left blank. The border is a formed by a single line.

Later History
The work was subsequently reissued in Dutch, with the plan unchanged -
a. With the title *Historische Landbeschryvinge van Groot-Brittanjen, ofte Engelandt, Schotlant, en Yrlandt...*, published by Wilhelmus Goeree in **Middleburgh** in **1666**.[2]
b. A further edition, published by B. Bos in **Rotterdam** in **1685**.[3]

1. Stephen p.200 (1661). BL 796.a.5; Bod Gough Gen Top 93; CUL Syn.8.66.24; Nfk.Lib.; Castle; RCF.
2. BL 10348.aaa.6.
3. BL G.15851. The plan in this edition has a larger margin.

[11] PETER STENT   London   1662

NORWICH[1]   50 x 30 mm.

Source
The Norwich Plan is one of a number of small town plans in the left, top and right margins of a map of England and Wales (395 x 505 mm.), a separate publication entitled *A New Map of the Kingdome of England and Principality of Wales taken out of I.S, Printed and are to be Sold by Peter Stent*[2], *at the white Horse in Giltspurr Street without Newgat 1662.*

Description
The map acknowledges John Speed (I.S.) as its source, and its twenty nine marginal town plans are based on the plans in Speed's county maps. The Norwich plan is second from the bottom on the right side, between Ipswich and Cambridge. Although it may be based on Speed's plan of Norwich **[4]**, it is a very poor and sketchy representation of the city. It shows the cathedral, the castle and the city walls, but little other recognisable detail, not even the windmills which are usually a prominent feature of the small city plans.

Later History
The map was reissued, without any alteration to the Norwich plan, as follows -
a. Dated **1665**.
b. Main post roads added.
c. Dated **1665**, but with the imprint of John Overton 'neere S:^{t} Pulchers church'.
d. Dated **1673**.
e. Dated **1673**, but Overton's address is shown as 'at the White Horse without Newgate'.[3]

1. Not in Stephen. BL Maps 185.n.1.(1.); RCF. For details see Shirley, *British Isles*, 1988, p.133, where references are given for each of the states of the map.
2. Peter Stent was a London print and mapseller, active from c.1642 until he died from the plague in 1665. After his death his shop and business were acquired by John Overton.
3. Illustrated in Shirley, *British Isles*, 1988, p.134.

[12] CHRISTOPHER SAXTON   London   1665

NORWICH[1]   60 x 135 mm.

Source
The plan is in the top right corner of a revised edition of Christopher Saxton's map of the county of Norfolk of 1574 (335 x 490 mm.). The map was extensively revised in 1665, when a plan of

the city was added. It appears that a further edition of Saxton's *Atlas* was planned, and a number of the county plates were revised.[2] However no edition was published at this time; following further revisions in c.1689, the date 1665 can still just be seen on the Norfolk map under the title, but no copy of the map in its 1665 form has been found. The map incorporating the Norwich plan is therefor first seen in the edition of Saxton's atlas published by Philip Lea in c.1689 under the title *All the Shires of England and Wales Described by Christopher Saxton Being the Best and Original Mapps With Many Additions and Corrections by Philip Lea. Sold by Philip Lea at the Atlas and Hercules in Cheapside near Friday Street and at his shop in Westminster Hall near the Court of Common Pleas.....*

Description (State 1)
The plan of the city is a close copy of the plan of Speed [4], but because it is smaller it has the appearance of being more crowded. The windmills and the river below the city extend into the borders. The title is below the plan, at the top of the panel containing references (30 x 95 mm.), which are directly copied from Speed. The border of the plan is a thin double line. The plan does not include the coat of arms of the city, or a compass indicator.

Later History
The plan of the city was revised (State 2) for the next edition of the *Atlas* published by Philip Lea in **c.1693**; it then appears without any further alteration in all subsequent editions of the *Atlas*, the last being that published by C. Dicey and Co. in **c.1770**.

Description (State 2)
The arms of the city have been added to the plan (with the heraldic colours indicated), and the city plan and the table of references are all surrounded by an additional new single line.

1. Stephen p. 201 (1690), p. 253 (1720), in need of revision. BL C.21.e.10; Bod Douce Prints b.28; Nfk.Lib.; RCF.
2. Discussed in Skelton, *County Atlases*, p. 121; I. M. Evans and H. Lawrence, *Christopher Saxton Elizabethan Map Maker,* Wakefield and London, 1979, p. 155.

[13] JOHN SPEED (2)   London   c.1666

NORWICHE[1]   100 x 170 mm.

Source
The plan of the city is in the top right corner of the map of the county of Norfolk, being a revised version of the map first engraved in 1610 for John Speed's *The Theatre of the Empire of Great Britain*. The new plate carries the signature of John Goddard, and the imprint of *Roger Rea at the Golden Cross in Cornhill against the Royall Exchange*. The map appears to have been produced in anticipation of the issue of a new edition of Speed's *Theatre*, but the map in this form has only been found as a loose sheet without text.

Description
The plan is a sharply engraved very close copy of the earlier Speed plan [4]. The slightly larger area allows the decorated panel containing the title to be separated from the border of the map, but in other respects the two are virtually identical.

Later History
A number of further editions of Speed's *Theatre* were issued between **1676** (with the imprint of

Bassett and Chiswell) and **1770** (with the imprint of C. Dicey and Co.), and separate copies of the map are also found without text. However no further alterations were made to the Norwich plan.[2]

1. Stephen p.201 (1666,1676); p.210 (1743), and the county maps referred to by Chubb, in need of revision. BL Maps C.7.e.6.(44.); Bod B1.14.Jur; Nfk.Lib.; Castle; RCF.
2. For details of the editions of Speed's *Theatre* see Skelton, *County Atlases,* and Hodson, *County Atlases,* 1984.

Illustration Plate 2

[14] ROBERT WALTON   **London**   **1668**

NORWICH[1]   30 x 50 mm.

Source
Norwich is one of a total number of thirty very small plans (including a view of London on fire in 1666) bordering a map of England and Wales (395 x 495 mm.) entitled *A New Map of England and Wales In Which the roads and Highways are playnly laid forth.....by T P* [Thomas Porter] *1668*. The separate imprint reads *Printed Colloured and sould by Rob Walton at the Dyall in Little Brittaine with all Other mapps.*[2]

[14] 1668 Robert Walton

**By permission of the British Library
Maps *1175 (117)**

Description
The map, and the Norwich plan, are very similar to those of Peter Stent **[11]**. There are thirteen small town plans along the right hand border, Norwich being sixth from the bottom, between Nottingham and Exeter. The title is within the rectangular border, above the view of the city. This is the least adequate of the small border representations of the city. The cathedral is prominent, and the city walls well defined, but other details are barely recognisable. As with the Stent plan, the windmills are absent, as is the portrayal of the river on its way towards Yarmouth.

Later History
A second edition of the map, without any change to the plan, was later issued with the omission of the reference to T P, and of the original date. Walton's address has been changed, and is now *at the Globe and Compasses at ye West end of St. Pauls in turning to Ludgate,* where he was in business between 1673 and 1676.[3]

1. Not in Stephen. BL Maps *1175 (117); Bod Sutherland 69 (VIII). See Shirley *British Isles*,1988, p.147, with illustration.
2. Robert Walton, 1618 - 1688, London printer, and print and mapseller. For details of his business career see Skelton, *County Atlases*, p.89, and Tyacke, *London Map-sellers*, p.145.
3. Illustrated in *The Map Collector,* March 1980, p.37.

[15] JOHANN CHRISTOPH BEER   Nuremberg   1690

Norwich:NORDOVICUM[1]   165 x 130 mm.

Source
From *Das neu-geharnischte Gross-Britannien, das ist: wahre Landes- und Standes Beschaffenheit derer drey-vereinigten Königreiche Engel- Schott- und Irrlands ...Nürnberg: in Verlegung Joh. Andreae Endtters seel. Sohne, 1690.*[2] This work, which is without text, contains 23 plans or views of British towns and cities, of which Norwich is one.[3]

Description
This is another small Norwich plan owing its origin ultimately to the plan of Cuningham [1]. It is a very close copy of the plan of Hermannides [10], on which it appears to have been based. Although small, the engraving is clear and detailed, showing the city walls and gates, the street pattern and the principal buildings. The two windmills are prominent, as are the roads beyond Bishop Bridge, and the river (without its name) extending to the top margin. Above the city is the title in a scroll, with the city arms (correctly shown) in a shield with an ornamental surround.

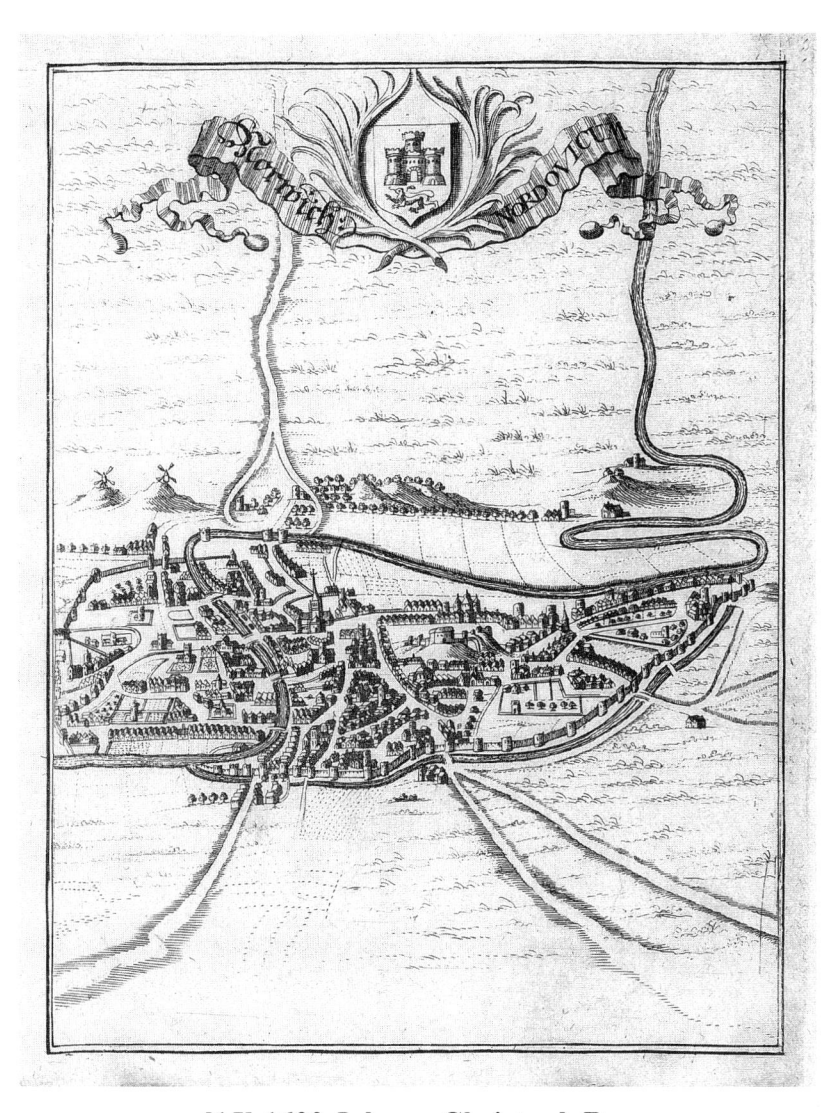

[15] 1690 Johann Christoph Beer

Later History There appear to be no later editions of the work. However the British Library has a small leather bound volume with *Plans of 17 Towns in Great Britain*, which includes the Norwich plan by Beer, and which appears to have been a separate compilation.[3]

1. Stephen p.201 (1690). BL 577.f.2.; BL Add. MS 23057.f.4; CUL F.169.c.1.1; Nfk.Lib.; RCF.
2. By Johann Christoph Beer (otherwise Baer or Bear), 1673-1753.
3. BL Maps C.27.e.3.

[16] THOMAS CLEER (1) London 1696

A TRUE and Exact MAPP of the Ancient and Famous CITY of NORWICH in y^e County of Norfolk. An ° 1696.[1]

1170 x 925 mm.

A Scale of 100 yards = 1.812" (45 mm.)   1:1987   31.89" = 1 mile

Source
A separate publication, with the imprint of *Tho. Cleer*.[2]

Origin of the Plan
The plan, which is the first professionally surveyed scale plan of the city, appears to have been a speculative production on the part of Thomas Cleer. There were no printers in Norwich capable of undertaking a work of this kind, and Cleer therefore had the plan engraved and printed in London, but arranged for its sale by local booksellers. A letter from a Norwich bookseller suggests that the plan (and the single sheet version **[17]**) was not produced in large numbers, and only a few copies were sold.[3] This seems to be confirmed by the rarity of the plan; the only copies which have been traced are two which are in Norwich.

Description
The plan is clearly engraved, and is printed on four numbered sheets. It shows the streets within the city walls, with drawings of the principal buildings, including the castle, cathedral, churches, the New Hall, the Duke's Palace and the Market Cross; other properties along street frontages are indicated conventionally without detail. The line of the walls and the gates are prominently shown, but do not appear to have been surveyed in detail. There are boats on the river. The dedication, top right, and below his coat of arms, is to *The High Puissant and Most Noble Prince Henry Duke of Norfolke*, to which have been added his numerous other titles.[4] The arms of the city are above the title of the map, bottom right; below, and to the right of a compass star, is a figure with dividers measuring from a scale on a tripod.

1. Stephen p. 201, (1696), with illustration. Nfk.Lib.(ex Norfolk and Norwich Archaeological Society Library); Castle.
2. Thomas Cleer is known to have been working as a surveyor during the period 1685 to 1706, on a variety of commissions, mainly in the south east, and was employed by the Crown in 1705. He is not known to have had any other connections with Norfolk. See Bendall, *Dictionary of Land Surveyors;* A.S.Mason, *Essex on the Map*, Chelmsford, 1990, p.32.
3. BL Add. MS 72703 S. The letter dated 13 July 1698 at Norwich is from George Rose, a Norwich Stationer, to George Moore, merchant, 'next dore to ye Golden Balls in Mansell Street in Goodman's Fields' -
'Yours and Mr. Cleer's Letters to my self and Mr Olliver [also a Norwich stationer and bookseller] about our Norwich Mapp per last Post I received. And accordingly (Mr. Olliver and his wife being out of Towne) I left your Note with his Sister for him. Since when hee is come home, but comes not at me. I am not certaine of what number

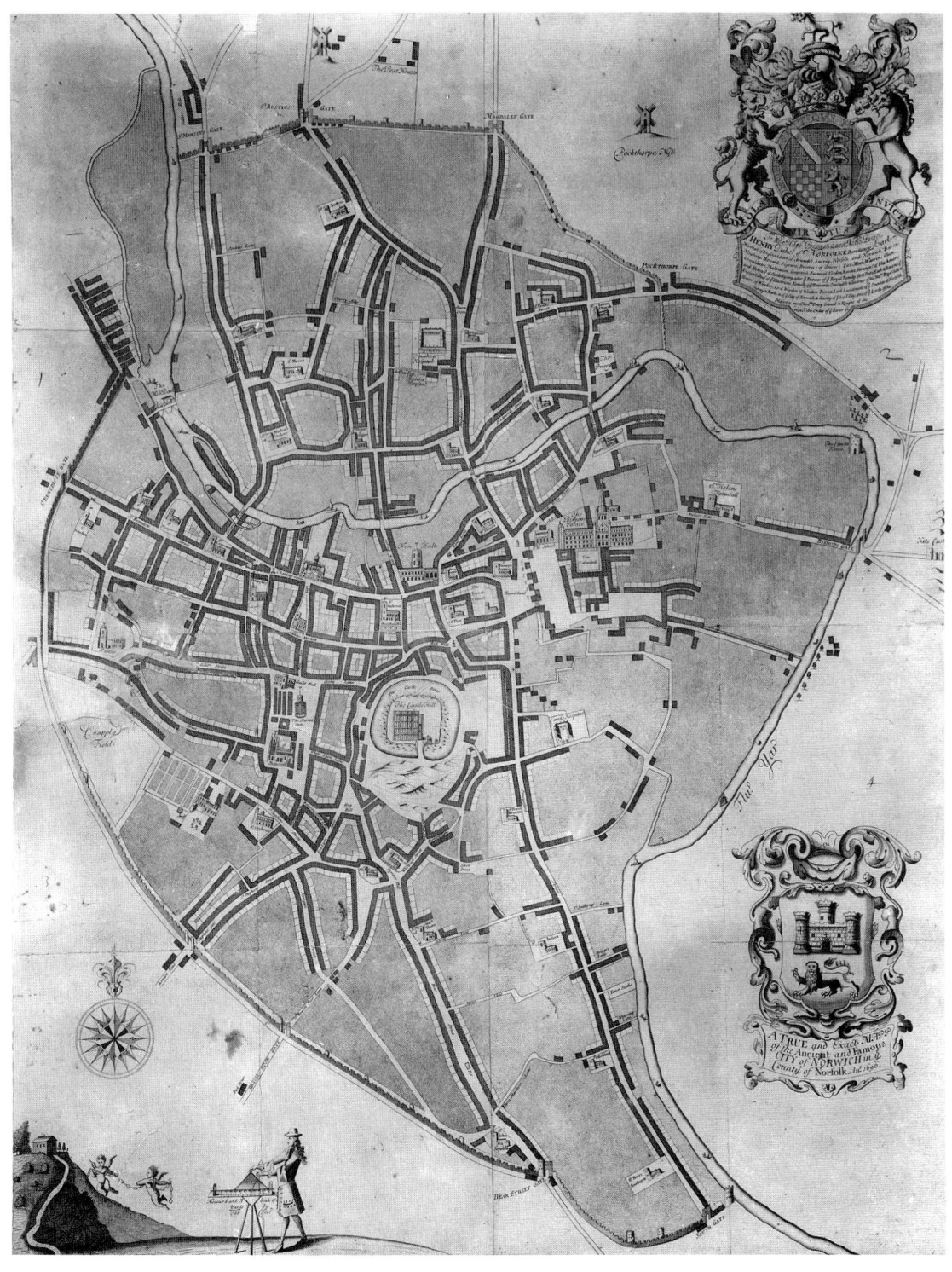

[16] 1696 Thomas Cleer (the four sheet plan)

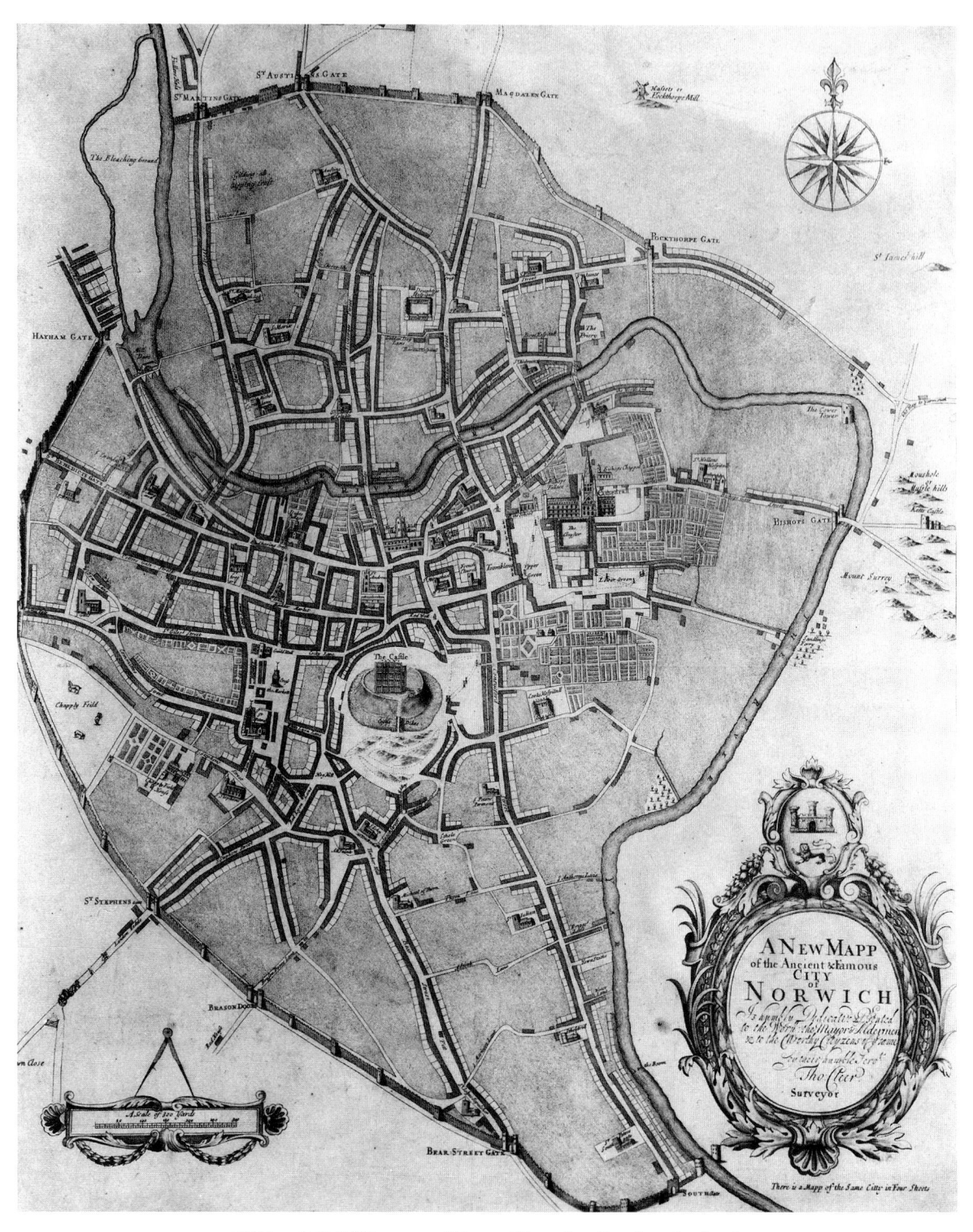

[17] c.1696 Thomas Cleer (the single sheet plan)

of the large Mapps I've Sold: Nor have I now time to count ye unsold; but well remember I never Sold but I pasted together, at 3^s. o r 3^s. 6^d. And I think but 6 or 7 Sheets at 2^s. 6^d. Each Map. And as yett but 3 of the new Small Size at 18^d. each. Nor do I advise you to send me above a dozen or 20 at the most of the small Mapps; because, notwithstanding all my Care & Industry to promote ye Sale thereof, they will not Sell in this Place, or at most, not for above 12d. a Piece. Nor do I think it worth while to trouble my self with any thing of slow Sale for 2d in the Shilling profitt. . Therefore had rather you'd think of some other Person & consequently discharge your Freind. Geo: Rose'

A postscript adds 'Many of the Large Mapps as well Pasted as in Sheets are, & were torne when Deliver'd to me.' The letter is annotated as received 15 July, and answered 6 August, but the answer has not survived.

4. Henry Howard 7th Duke of Norfolk, 1655-1701, Lord Lieutenant of Norfolk. The Duke's Palace in Norwich was rebuilt by the 6th Duke, but not finished. The 7th Duke was the last Duke of Norfolk to live in the city, and the palace was substantially demolished in 1711.

[17]   THOMAS CLEER (2)   **London**   **c.1696**

A NEW Mapp of the Ancient CITY of NORWICH[1]   625 x 510 mm.

A Scale of 300 yards = 2.875" (73 mm.)   1:3754   16.88" = 1 mile

Source
A separate publication with the imprint of *Tho: Cleer*.[2]

Origin of the Plan
A reduced version produced by Thomas Cleer of his four sheet plan of the city **[16]**. It is not dated, but under the title is a reference to the larger plan *There is a Mapp of the same city in four sheets*. Both were being sold in Norwich in 1698 (see **[16]** note 3), and it seems likely that the issue of the smaller plan followed very shortly after the issue of the larger in 1696 or 1697.

Description
While Cleer's smaller plan is generally very similar to his four sheet plan, there are a number of significant alterations. The most obvious is the addition of garden layouts in the Cathedral Close, in an area to the south of the Close and fronting Kings Street, and also gardens of properties between St.Giles Street and Committee Street (now Bethel Street). Other differences are comparatively minor. They include a reference to The Mint at the New Hall (now St. Andrew's Hall); a mint was established in the city in 1696, and operated for the next two years. The walls and gates are redrafted in a somewhat stylised form. There are no boats on the river, which is given the name 'Yar'.

1. Stephen p. 202 (c.1696). Bod Gough Maps Norfolk 3; Castle; RCF.
2. See notes under **[16]**.

[18] VINCENZO CORONELLI (1)   **Venice**   **1706**

NORWICH, Latinis. NORDOVCUM [1]   125 x 180 mm.

Source
From Volume 3 of a work entitled *Teatro della Guerra del P. Coronelli*, this volume having the

title *Isole Britanniche: Inghilterra, Scozia, Irlanda.*[2] The work has an Introduction in Italian. It contains a very large number of plans and other prints, and the composition may vary; in the copy in the British Library the two Norwich plans are numbered 38 and 39 in the index, whereas in the copy in the Bodleian they are numbered 139 and 132 respectively; the plans themselves are not numbered.

Description
A sketchily drawn plan, which has been copied from that of Hermannides [10]. Within wide margins the plan has a double two line border. As with the plan of Hermannides, and also that of Beer [15] the road and river extend to the top margin, but the river is not named. The two windmills are again a prominent feature. The city coat of arms is correctly shown, top left, and the title within a double line border is in the top right corner. The back is plain.

1. Not in Stephen. BL C.44.f.6; Bod G.A. Oxon 4^0 10 ; Nfk.Lib.; RCF.
2. Vincenzo Maria Coronelli, 1650-1718, was ordained as a Franciscan priest, and became Father General of his order in 1699. He spent most of his life in Venice, where he was appointed Cartographer to the Venetian Republic. He was famous as a theologian, mathematician, cartographer and globe maker.

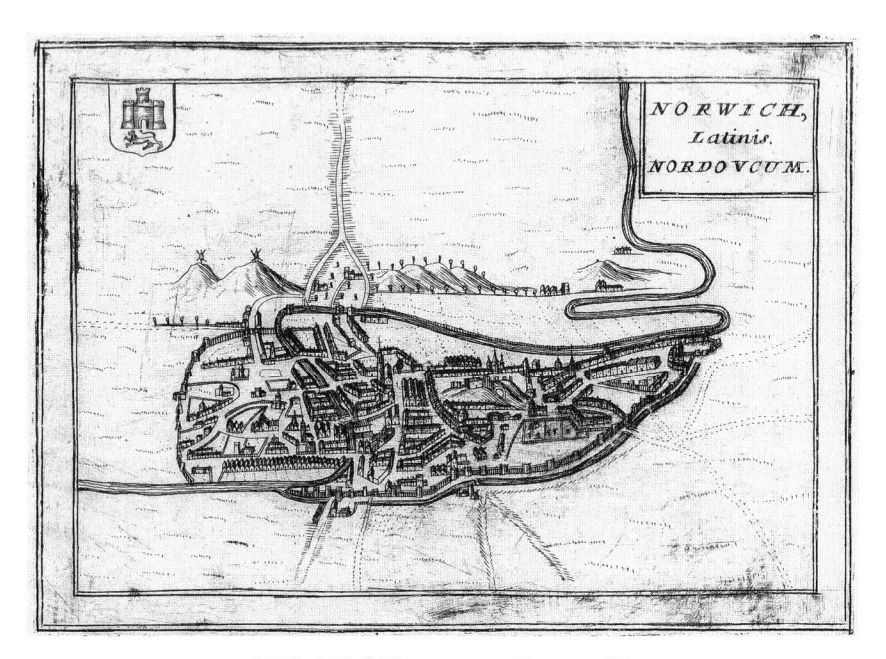

[18] 1706 Vincenzo Coronelli

[19] VINCENZO CORONELLI (2)　　　　　　　　　　　　Venice　　　1706

NORDWICH, CAPITAL DEL CONTADO DI NORFOLCK[1]　　　　125 x 180 mm.

Source
From the same work as [18].

Description
Although from the same work as the other plan of Coronelli, the plan has considerable differences, both in title and appearance, and one wonders if the compiler appreciated that they were of the same town. The city is recognizable by its outline, the walls being prominent,

but within the city much of the detail is different, the castle has disappeared, and the cathedral is only just visible. There are no windmills. The plan appears to be based on that of Valezo [3], and as with the plans of Valezo and of Meisner [9] the city arms are reversed.

1. Not in Stephen. See [18] note 1, for copies in the British Library and the Bodleian; Nfk.Lib.; RCF.

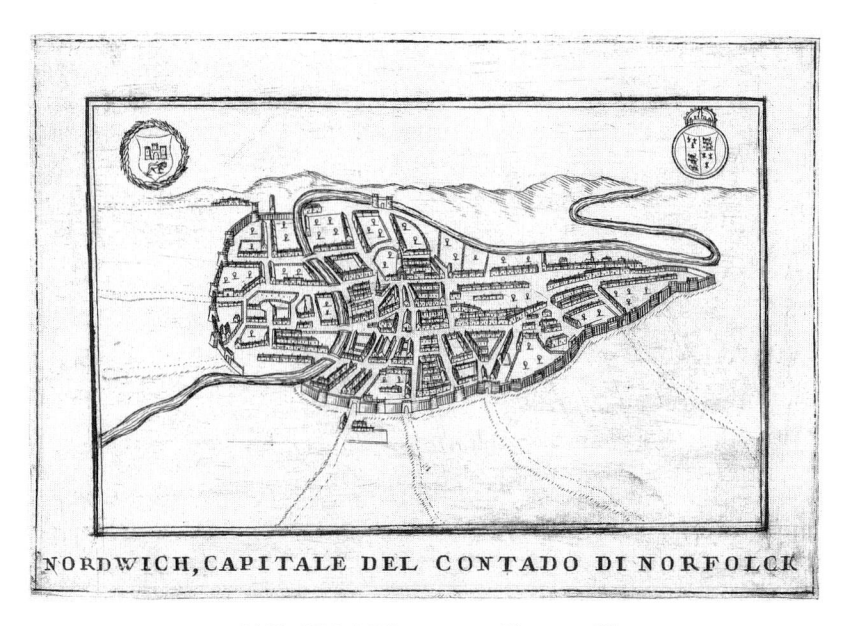

[19] 1706 Vincenzo Coronelli

[20] **SUTTON NICHOLLS** London c.1710

Norwich[1] 250 x 175 mm.

A Scale of 400 yards = 1.375" (35 mm.) 1:10473 6.05" = 1 mile

Source
The source of this plan, which is only known from one example in the British Library, has not been established.

Description
A clearly engraved plan, with almost exactly the same detail as that shown by the smaller plan of Cleer [17]. The title is in a scrolled cartouch top right, with the city arms top left. To the right of the river is a compass indicator, and references to the cathedral and the city churches. Below the city is the scale bar, and within the bottom border, formed by a thick outer and thin inner line, is the imprint of the engraver *Sutton Nicholls sculp.*[2]

1. Stephen p. 203 (1710); BL Maps K.Top.31.30.
2. Sutton Nicholls was a London draughtsman and engraver, with a prolific output, which included maps in the reissue of Saxton's *Atlas* in c.1689, Camden's *Britannia* in 1695, and many other maps and illustrations for books of many kinds. They include a plan of Exeter in 1724, and prospects of a number of towns; it seems possible that Nicholls' plan of Norwich was intended for inclusion in some other publication, but no such publication has been traced. The Norwich plan is listed in *The Norfolk Topograher's Manual* under the date 1718, but this appears to be a reference to the copy in the British Library mentioned above..

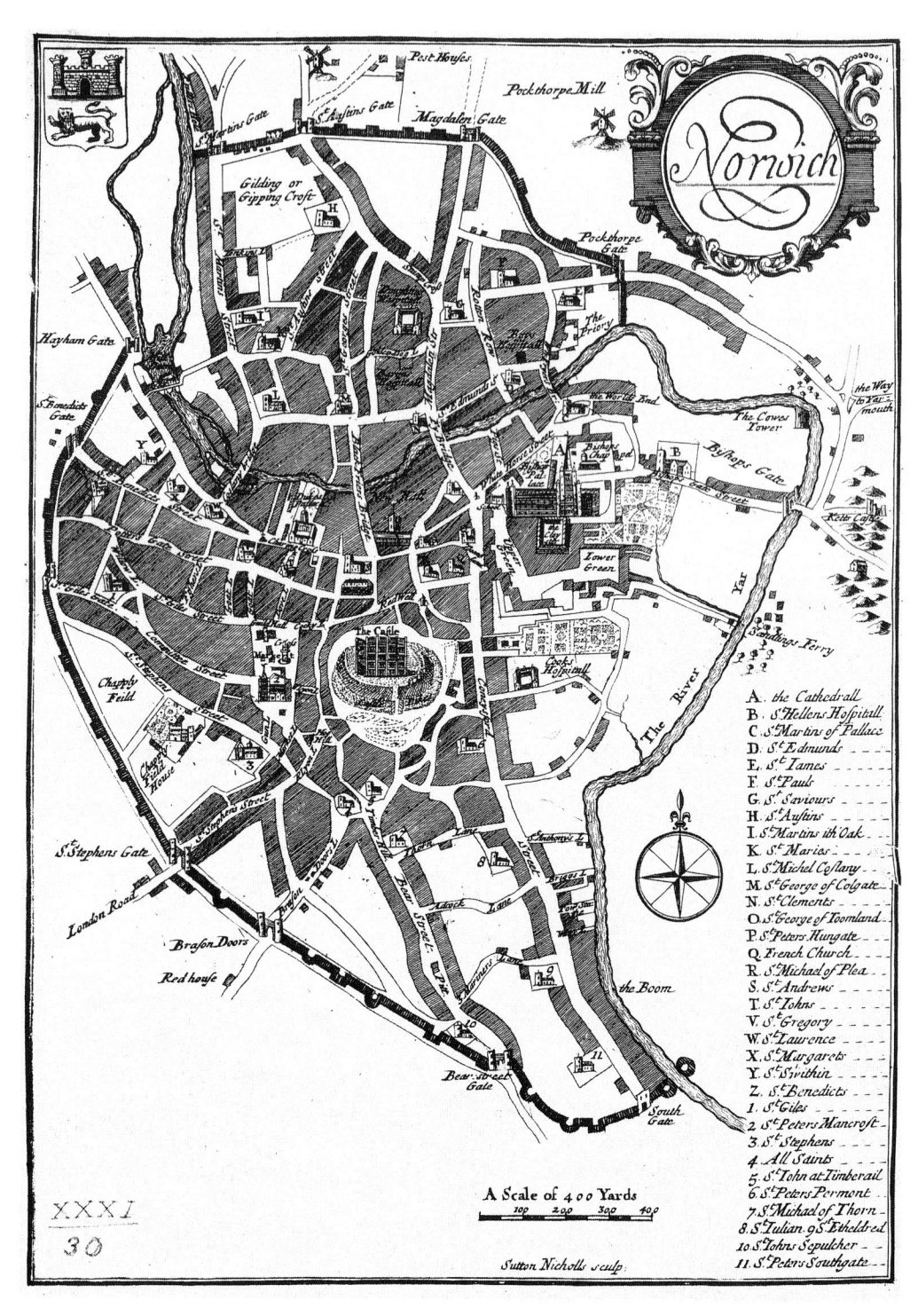

[20] c.1710 Sutton Nicholls
By permission of the British Library Maps K.Top.31.30

[21] JOHN HOYLE   Norwich   1720

A NEW MAPP of the CITY of NORWICH[1]   215 x 177 mm.

A Scale of 300 yards = 1.06" (27 mm.)   1:4800   (6.23" = 1 mile)

Source
The plan, engraved by John Hoyle,[2] was originally produced as a separate publication for sale by the Norwich bookseller Thomas Goddard.[3] It was subsequently used to accompany *A Compleat History of the Famous City of Norwich. From the Earliest Account, to this present Year of 1728.... To which is annexed an Exact Map of the City...Norwich: Printed and Sold by William Chase in the Cockey Lane, 1728.*[4] This *History* is the first of the city containing a plan, and was also published with a London imprint *Printed for John and James Knapton, Booksellers, in St. Paul's Church-yard, MDCCXXVIIII.I I.*[5]
The plan was also issued by William Chase on a separate sheet, above text with the heading *A Geographical and Historical Description of the City of Norwich, from its first Original to this Time, as taken from the General Atlas, with Additions.*[6]

Description (State 1)
The plan is a reduced version of the smaller plan of Cleer [17], on which it appears to have been based - see for instance the name of the river 'Yar', and the spelling of 'Toombland'. Above the road leading from the city outside St. Stephen's Gate are the words 'Ikning Street', perhaps a corruption of the word 'Icknield', but not a name of the road found elsewhere.[7] The border is formed by a thick outer and thin inner line. Below the top border is the title, and top right a compass indicator and the scale; bottom right is the list of references to the churches and other buildings; bottom left are the city arms in an ornamental cartouch, with the name of the engraver *IOHN HOYLE Sculp.*[8]

Description (State 2)
The words 'Ikning Street' have been deleted.

Later History
The copper plate of the plan came into the possession of Samuel Woodward, and afterwards one James Mills.[9] A number of impressions were taken from the plate in the early 19th century, and can be identified by the comparative lightness of the printing, and the difference in the paper.[10]

1. Stephen pp. 207, 208 (1728); p. 220 (1822). BL 291.e.15; BL Add. MS 23037.f.35; Bod Gough Maps Norfolk 12 and 13; CUL Maps bb.77.72.1 Nfk.Lib.; Castle; RCF.
2. The identity of John Hoyle has not been established. It seems more than likely that he was local to Norwich, and a family with the name of Hoyle was living in the city at this period. A John Hoyle was admitted freeman (as 'haberdasher of hats') on 27 November 1719; another John was admitted freeman (as a 'woolcomber') on 27 April 1723; a John was constable in 1720, perhaps the John (referred to as 'Senior') who was a city councillor from 1731 to 1744; and a John, described as 'Citizen', died aged 82 in 1747. A family of some standing in the city such as this would have been well known to Thomas Goddard and to William Chase, and it seems very probable that one of the Johns was asked by Goddard to engrave the plan for him. No professional engravers have been recorded in the city at this time. For Thomas Goddard see [28], note 2.
3. The first reference to the plan is in *The Norwich Gazette* of 5th November 1720 - ' On Monday the 14th of this Instant November will be published a curious exact map of the City of Norwich engraved upon new Copper-Plate by Mr. John Hoyle, wherein are exactly described all the churches.......(etc.)   Price 2d. Sold by Mr. Goddard Bookseller in the Market Place.'
4. For Willliam Chase see *Norwich Mercury* [24], note 2.

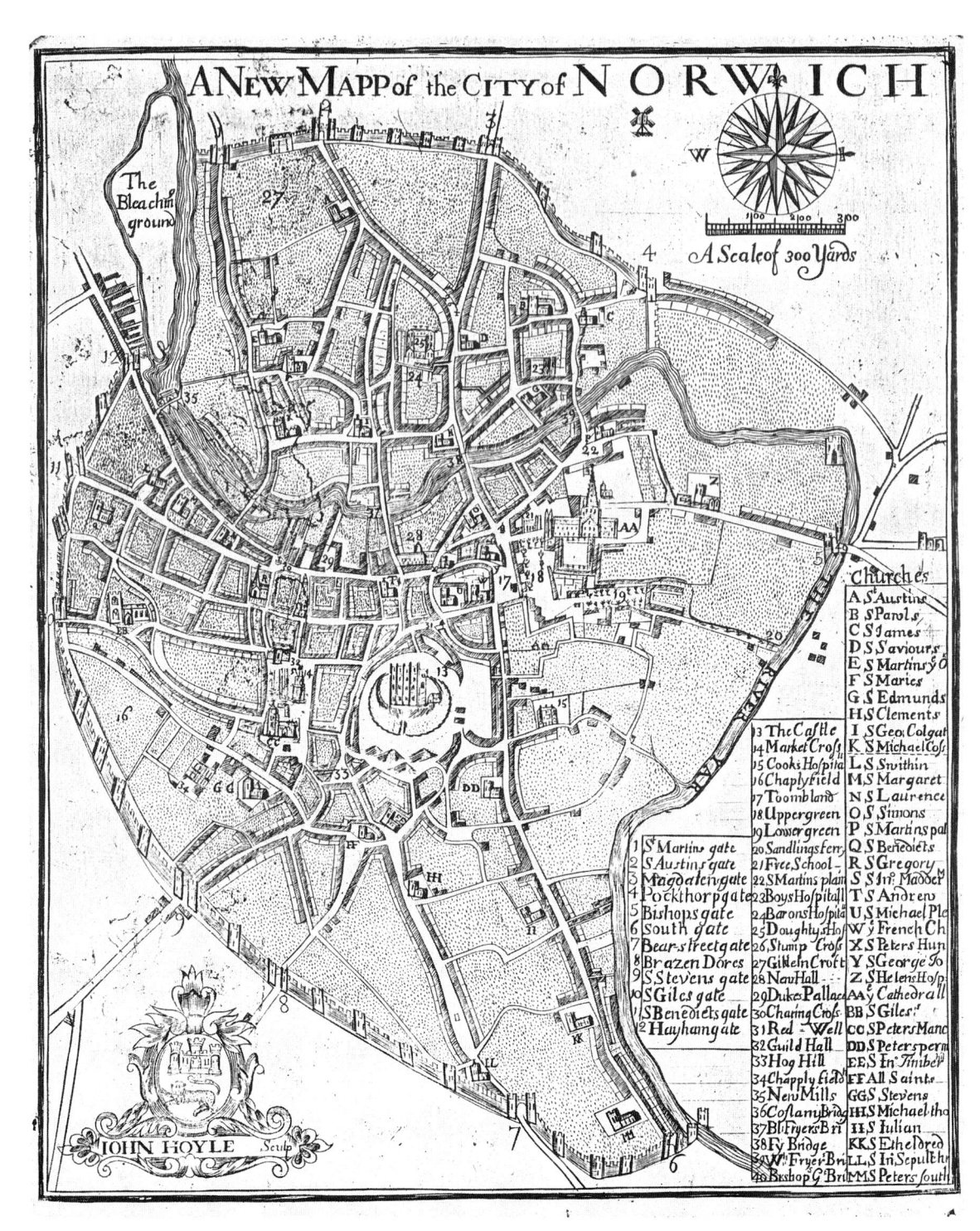

[21] 1720 (1728) John Hoyle

5. The London imprint is spurious, and perhaps used by Chase with a view to making the book more marketable; the use by larger provincial printers of false London imprints appears to have been a fairly common practice; see David Stoker, op. cit., [24], note 3.
6. Two settings of the text are known, with different initial letters, one with 18 lines and one with 19 lines; the imprint *Sold by W. Chase in the Cockey Lane. Price 3d.* was printed below the text, although in surviving copies this is often found to be missing.
7. The only copy of the plan seen by the author in State 1, which includes the name of the road, is Bod Gough Maps Norfolk 14. All other copies are in State 2.
8. On the plan in a copy of the *History* in the author's and in another private collection the name of the engraver has been blocked out.
9. A note on a copy of the plan in the Norfolk and Norwich Archaeological Society library states 'Impression from a Copper Plate in the possession of Mr. Samuel Woodward, afterwards of Mr. James Mills and sold at his auction.' Samuel Woodward, antiquarian and geologist, author of, inter alia, *An Outline of the Geology of Norfolk* Norwich, 1833, and *The Norfolk Topographer's Manual* (see Introduction) published in 1842, after his death.
10. As mentioned in Stephen, a copy in Nfk.Lib. is printed on paper with the watermark 1822.

[22] THOMAS KIRKPATRICK (Prospect)   Norwich   1723

The North East Prospect of the CITY of NORWICH[1]   590 x 1510 mm.

Source
A separate publication, with the imprints outside the bottom border, left *T.Kirkpatrick delin,*[2] and right *E.Kirkall sculp.*[3] The Dedication, which is to Viscount Townshend,[4] is signed by Thomas Kirkpatrick.

Origin of the Prospect
Although the Prospect was drawn by Thomas Kirkpatrick, it seems likely that the inspiration for it will have come from his brother John, who already had a reputation as a keen antiquary. Proposals for printing the Prospect were issued dated August 24, 1723; Thomas's name did not appear, and subscriptions were to be received by John Kirkpatrick in St. Andrew's Parish, and at Brathwait's Coffee House in the Market Place, price 3s., one half down and one half on delivery. The Proposals refer to the original drawing having been viewed by several competent judges in Norwich and in London, and it was shown to the Society of Antiquaries in London on 11 December 1723.[5] The Prospect was engraved in London by Elisha Kirkall, and notice of the publication appeared in the *Norwich Gazette* in the issue of 12 December 1724. The notice was repeated in each of the next three issues, while the publication was also announced in London in the *London Journal* of 2 January 1724/5. While the Norwich announcements said that the Prospect was sold by 'the booksellers in Norwich and by Mr. John Kirkpatrick in St. Andrew's Parish', the London notice said that it was to be sold by 'Thomas Kirkpatrick, Linnen Draper at the Golden Ball in Lady Lane', the price to be 3s.6d. 'with reasonable Allowance to the Print-sellers'.

Description
A very detailed panoramic view of the city, as seen from a point on the hills on the north east. The angle of vision is such that the road pattern within the walls is not readily apparent, but nevertheless the line of the walls can be traced, and the city within the walls is seen as a whole. All the gates are indicated, even on the far side of the city where they are not directly visible. The most prominent features are the cathedral, the castle, and the churches, all of which are carefully and individually drawn; much of the Prospect comprises the tightly packed rows of houses, most

[22] 1723 Thomas Kirkpatrick (Prospect)

of which are shown in a more or less standard form, but close study of the Prospect, assisted by the comprehensive 'Explanation', reveals many interesting details of the city both inside and outside the city walls.

Outside the walls, in the foreground on the northern side of the city, is the suburb of Pockthorpe. However, as shown on the earlier city plans, there was very little development beyond the walls, and the Prospect shows fields with cattle, and people harvesting; to the left is Mousehold, with references to Kett's camp, and the ruins of St. Michael's Chapel, 'commonly called Kett's Castle'; the windmill on the right, when viewed from the other side of the city, is a feature of Cuningham's and other early plans. In the distance beyond the city is the open countryside, extending on the south to Poringland windmill and the steeple of Hethersett church.

In the centre, above the actual Prospect, is the title, with the arms of the city, with supporters, and surmounted by the cap of maintenance; top left, supported by putti, are the arms of the diocese, and top right, similarly supported, are those of the deanery.

Beneath the view of the city is the dedication, and below the dedication Viscount Townshend's coat of arms. Bottom left is a panel containing illustrations of 'Some Pieces of Antient Silver Money' which were coined in the city;[6] bottom right is 'A Plan of the City of Norwich' (see **[23]**). The remainder of the lower section contains a comprehensive 'Explanation of the Prospect and Plan', in six sections: churches within the city then in use; parish churches demolished or decayed; monasteries, hospitals etc.; other remarkable buildings, gates tower etc.; and finally buildings or features 'Outside the City'. There then follows a further panel headed 'Norwich is also a County of it self' describing its boundaries.

Later History

It is not known how many copies of the Prospect were printed. Copies are rare, but a number have survived in Norwich, and in national collections. A full size photo-lithographic reproduction of the Prospect was issued in James Campbell, *Norwich,* The Scolar Press in conjunction with the Historic Towns Trust, London, 1975.[7]

1. Stephen p.204 (1723), and illustration, Plate XXII. BL Maps K.Top.31.34.a; Bod Gough Maps 24; Nfk.Lib.; Castle; RCF.
2. Thomas Kirkpatrick and his younger brother John were two of the sons of Thomas Kirkpatrick, a native of Closeburn in Dumfriesshire, who came to Norfolk to marry Ann Sendall in Haveringland in 1686. The family were living in St. Stephen's parish by 1691, and both Thomas and John were to play a significant role in the life of the city.
Thomas Kirkpatrick, ?c.1690 - 1755, is much less well known than his brother John. He is at one point described as a linen-draper, but if he served an apprenticeship this did not lead to his admission as a freemen. He was however granted the freedom of the city in 1732, in which year he was appointed city chamberlain, a position which he held until 1744. He was buried in St. Helen's Church in 1755.
John Kirkpatrick, 1687 - 1728, was apprenticed to Thomas Andrews as a linen-draper, and was admitted to the freedom of the city on 24 February 1710/11. He subsequently became a business partner of John Custance, sheriff of the city in 1723, and mayor in 1726 and again in 1750, and of the family later to feature in Parson Woodforde's Diaries. John himself was a councillor from 1719 to 1727, and an auditor during this period. In 1726 he became Treasurer of the Great Hospital, and at following his death in 1728 at the early age of 42 he was buried in St. Helen's, the Hospital Church.
John was an indefatigable antiquarian, and a leading member of a group with similar interests known as the Society of Icenians; they included Benjamin Mackerell, city librarian and historian, see Goddard and Chase **[28]**, note 3. John amassed a substantial library, and accumulated a vast amount of historical material, which however had not been published prior to his death. By his will John left all his books, manuscripts and material relating to the history of Norwich to his brother Thomas, with the hope that they might be published, and after Thomas's death they were to be given to the city. Some of the notes had been copied by Thomas and were used by Blomefield for his *History of Norfolk*, but many of his notes were eventually published during the 19th century. Of particular importance are *History of the Religious Orders and Communities, and of the Hospitals and Castle, of Norwich,*

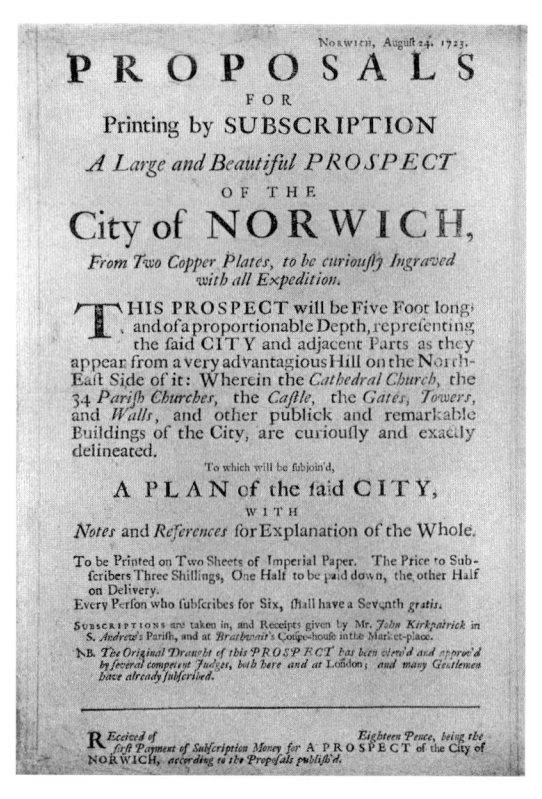

[22] 1723 Thomas Kirkpatrick (Prospect)
Proposals for Printing by Subscription

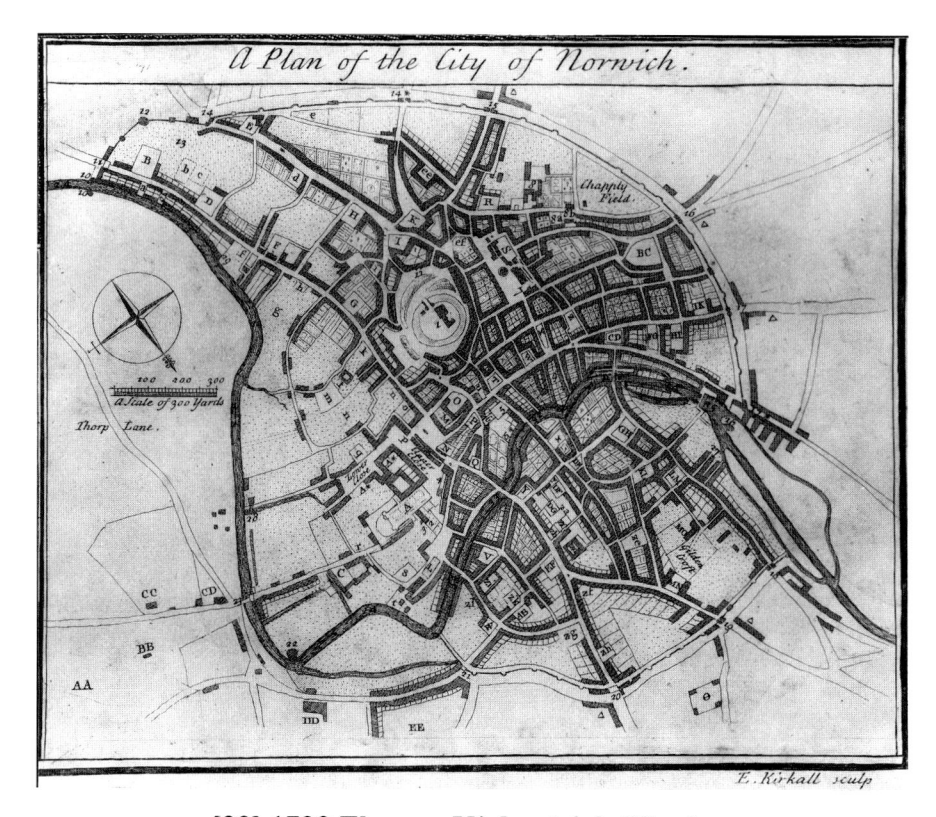

[23] 1723 Thomas Kirkpatrick (Plan)

Edwards and Hughes, London, and Stevenson and Matchett, Norwich, 1845, and *The Streets and Lanes of the City of Norwich*, Norfolk and Norwich Archaeological Society, Norwich, 1889.
3. Elisha Kirkall, a prominent London engraver, of Wine Office Court, Fleet Street. His wide variety of work, advertised from time to time in the *Norwich Gazette*, included a large scale four sheet map of Warwickshire, 1728.
4. Charles, Second Viscount Townshend, 1674-1738, Baron Townshend of Lynn Regis, a Principal Secretary of State, and Lord Lieutenant of the County of Norfolk and of the County of the City of Norwich; one of the most powerful figures in the country at this period, known to posterity as 'Turnip' Townshend. Extensive literature, e.g. James M. Rosenheim, *The Townshends of Raynham*, Wesleyan University Press, Middletown, Connecticut, 1989, Susanna Wade Martins, *"Turnip" Townshend Statesman and Farmer*, Poppyland Publishing, North Walsham, 1990.
5. The Minutes of the Society record that Thomas Kirkpatrick was permitted to show the design, 'and thereupon several Fellows present subscribed for it'.
6. Certain of the coins are stated to have been owned John Kirkpatrick, who on his death left a collection of coins to his brother Thomas and then to the city. These seem subsequently to have disappeared
7. Although not itself reprinted, reduced versions of the Prospect include those on the county maps of Norfolk by Corbridge [27], Goddard and Chase [28], Foster [29] and Goddard and Goodman [30], and later as separate publications, [38] and [39].

[23]   THOMAS KIRKPATRICK (Plan)   Norwich   1723

A Plan of the City of Norwich[1]   180 x 220 mm.

Scale 300 yards = 1" (26 mm.)   1:10794   5.87" = 1 mile

Source
The plan comprises the bottom right corner panel of Kirkpatrick's *Prospect* [22].

Origin of the Plan
Although the plan forms an integral part of Thomas Kirkpatrick's *Prospect,* there is little doubt that it is in fact the work of John. The original drawing of the plan is in the same style as other drawings which are known to be by him, and its content is consistent with John's known interest in the gates and walls and the streets and lanes of the city.

Description
The plan is unusual in its orientation, with south-south-west to the top; there is a compass indicator to the left of the river on the eastern side of the city. The plan itself has been finely drawn and engraved, and although it appears to have been based on the smaller plan of Cleer [17],[2] it has a number of features which indicate that it is not merely a reduced copy of that plan.[3] Many buildings are referred to in the 'Explanation', which relates both to the the *Prospect* and to the plan, and the city walls are now drawn with their gates and bastions in much more detail.[4] The title is in a narrow panel above the plan.

1. Bod Gough Maps Norfolk 8. The original manuscript drawing is in the Castle, part of the Fitch Collection.
2. It is known that John Kirkpatrick had copies of both the Cleer plans; his annotated copy of the large plan [16], is held by the Castle, and his copy of the smaller plan is referred to by Stephen p. 203.
3. For instance Surrey House in present day Surrey Street ('ee' on the plan) is shown and named for the first time.
4. John Kirkpatrick made drawings of the city gates in 1720, which were engraved by Henry Ninham and published with a short explanatory text in 1864.

[24] NORWICH GAZETTE					Norwich						1725

[THE Norwich Gazette][1]							57 x 195 mm.

Source
The prospect heads the top of the front page of the weekly newspaper *The Norwich Gazette*, from the issue (number 969) of 1 May 1725[2] to the issue (number 1944) of 7 January 1744. The newspaper was owned and printed by Henry Cross-Grove in St. Giles Parish, Norwich.[3]

Description
The prospect is based on the North East Prospect of Kirkpatrick [22] which had recently been published. In the foreground is the city wall, with an impression of closely packed buildings. The large windmill which is a prominent feature of Kirkpatrick's prospect is missing. The buildings on the skyline, in particular the cathedral, the castle and the churches, are readily recognizable, but only to a very limited extent the pattern of the streets. The title of the newspaper is above the prospect, with a small panel with Saint George to the left, and the Norwich city arms to the right.

[24] 1725 (1730) The Norwich Gazette

1. Not in Stephen. The only surviving copy of the *Gazette* for May 1725 which has been traced is in the BL, Newspaper Library. Later copies, including those for 1744, are in Nfk.Lib.
2. Although issues of the *Gazette* for the early months of 1725 have not survived, the adoption of this heading seems to have resulted from a change in the format of the newspaper, consequent upon the passing of the Stamp Act 1725 (11 Geo. c. 8). The Act came into effect on 26 April 1725, and imposed a duty of 1/2d. on each sheet of paper. Although an earlier Stamp Act had likewise imposed a duty on each sheet of paper, this had been largely avoided by newspapers being issued as pamphlets, thus incurring a single payment instead of duty on each sheet. The 1725 Act threatened to make the local newspapers uneconomic, but they realised that they could limit the duty to 1/2d. by printing on a single sheet, which was then folded to produce a four page paper. Each weekly issue is now in this form, and carries a red 1/2d. stamp showing that the duty had been paid. See G.A.Cranfield, *The Development of the Provincial Newspaper*, Oxford, 1962, (reprinted Westport, Connecticut, 1978).
3. Henry Cross-Grove, 1683-1744, was one of the leading printers and booksellers in Norwich in the first part of the 18th century. Having come from London, he took over the printing of *The Norwich Gazette* for Samuel Hasbart, a member of a prominent Norwich business family. The first issue of the newspaper was on 7 December 1706, from which subsequent issues were numbered. He took over completely from Hasbart in 1718, and continued as proprietor and printer until his death, when he was succeeded by his widow and his son-in-law. For his rivalry with William Chase see *The Norwich Mercury* [25].

[25] NORWICH MERCURY　　　　　　　　　　　Norwich　　　　　　　　　　1726

[THE Norwich Mercury][1]　　　　　　　　　　　　　　　　　54 x 192 mm.

Source

The heading at the top of the front page of the weekly newspaper *The Norwich Mercury* from the issue of 12 February 1726 to the issue of 27 December 1740. The newspaper was owned and printed by William Chase in the Cockey Lane (now London Street) Norwich.[2]

Description

The inspiration for this view of Norwich was clearly Kirkpatrick's Prospect [22]. It gives a very crowded appearance of the city, but the major features are the city wall in the foreground, and against the skyline the cathedral (to the left of the title), the castle, and a number of identifiable churches. It is similar to the version of the prospect adopted by *The Norwich Gazette* [24], but extends over a rather smaller area; prominent on the left is a windmill, not the windmill on the Kirkpatrick Prospect which is to the right. The decorative plate has, above the prospect, the title of the newspaper, the motto *Fama Volat*, and along the top small panels containing the arms of the city, the bishopric and the deanery, and St. George and the dragon.[3]

[25] 1726 (1738-39) The Norwich Mercury

1. Not in Stephen. BL; Nfk.Lib.
2. William Chase, 1692-1744, was a leading Norwich printer, publisher and bookseller. He was apprenticed to the Norwich bookseller Thomas Goddard (see [28]), for whom he continued to work until he was admitted a freeman on 24 February 1715/16. He had already set up in business as a bookseller on his own account in 1714 from premises in Dove Lane, but as a freeman bookseller he moved to larger premises in Cockey Lane (now London Street), and from there he took over from Goddard the publication of the weekly newspaper *The Norwich Mercury*. He served as a member of the city council from 1718 to 1727, and again from 1730 until his death. He was a strong supporter of the Whigs; his great rival Henry Cross-Grove, also a city councillor from 1728 to 1744, and publisher of the other weekly newspaper *The Norwich Gazette*, was equally strongly a supporter of the Tories, a feature of the two papers during this period being the often vitriolic, and what would nowadays be libellous, comments about each other in their respective newspapers. See David Stoker, *Prosperity and Success in the Eighteenth Century Book Trade: the Firm of William Chase & Co.*, in *Publishing History* 30, 1991.
3. A very curious feature is that from the issue of 20 April 1734 to the issue of 27 December 1740 the printing of the prospect has been reversed. The windmill is accordingly now on the right, and the spire of the cathedral is found to the right rather than to the left of the title. This appears to have happened without editorial comment. The other features of the heading have not been changed.

[26]   JAMES CORBRIDGE (Plan)   **London**   **1727**

MAPP OF THE CITY OF NORWICH[1]   700 x 1005 mm.

A Scale of 400 yards or 1200 feet = 3.875" (97mm.)   1:3716   17.05" = 1 mile

Source
A separate publication, dedicated to the Right Honourable Charles Townshend[2] by J.Corbridge,[3] and with imprints outside the bottom border, left, *I.Harris Sculp. in Water Street Bridwell Percint.*[4], and right, *Delin p^r J.Corbridge 1727*.

Origin of the Plan
In the *Norwich Gazette* of 1 August 1724 James Corbridge, Surveyor, advertised his proposal for the printing by subscription of surveys of Norwich, Great Yarmouth and King's Lynn. The price for each was to be 2s. down an 3s. on delivery, but those gentlemen who wished to have their houses or arms in the margins were asked to pay 7s. down and 3s. on delivery. He never produced a plan of King's Lynn, but went on to publish a fine prospect and plan of Great Yarmouth. The Norwich Plan is stated to have been drawn in the mayoralty of John Croshold (1724-25), although its completion was not finally announced until the end of 1727.[5] The plan is very similar in concept to the plan which Corbridge had produced of Newcastle-upon-Tyne,[6] a scale plan of the city, surrounded by drawings of principal buildings, and the houses of leading citizen. Corbridge went on to publish a map of the county of Norfolk containing a prospect of Norwich **[27]**, further maps of Norfolk and Suffolk, and a number of important surveys of country estates.

Description (State 1)
One of the most interesting of the earlier plans of Norwich, not so much for the actual plan of the city as for the surrounding drawings. The plan closely follows the smaller plan of Cleer **[17]**, on which it appears to have been based.[7] However it is the work of a professional surveyor; it has a more attractive finish, and where for instance Cleer has shown properties fronting streets merely in shaded block form, Corbridge has shown three dimensional buildings. The churches and other properties illustrated have been separately identified and drawn, and in the case of the private houses the names of the owners are given. Street, gate and other names generally follow those of Cleer (although 'Sandlings Ferry is wrongly shown as 'Sandleys Ferry'), but the the river through the city which Cleer called 'Yar' is shown by Corbridge as 'Yare or Wens Flu'. Sailing ships are shown on the river entering the city, with a note '32 miles to Yarmouth Navigable For Keeles of 40 or 50 Tunns. Here is Likewise Night and Day Wherrys Verry Convenient for Passengers'.
Beneath the plan is a compass rose, with the scale bar below. Along the bottom are references to the division of the city into wards, and a section about the bishopric. The central panel refers to the mayoralty of John Croshold, and contains the dedication. There follows a short section about the city, including references to its latitude of 52.42, its two members of parliament, Robert Britiffe and Waller Bacon, its 7,000 houses, and its population of 42,000.
Around the plan of the city are drawings of its principal public buildings, the castle, the guildhall, and the cathedral, thirty five city churches, and the houses of fifteen leading citizens.[8]

Later History
Although the plan was published in Norwich in 1727, no copies with an original publisher's imprint have been seen. Corbridge said in his proposals that the plate would be engraved when

[26] 1727 James Corbridge (Plan)

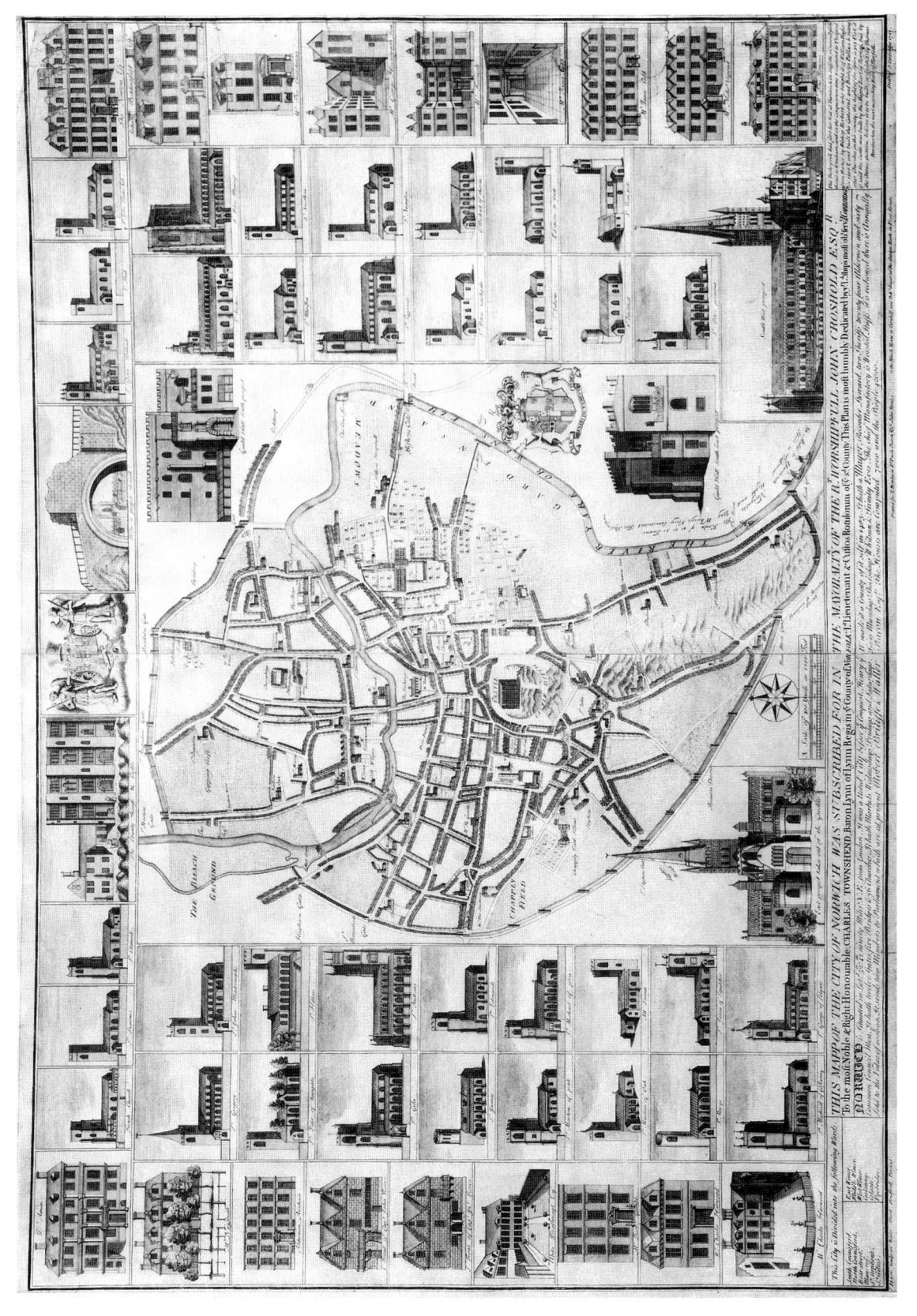

he had three hundred subscriptions, but the conclusion to be drawn seems to be that there were comparatively few original sales. However the plates survived and came into the possession of London publishers; the plan was advertised for sale in John Bowles' catalogue of 1768, and Sayer and Bennett's catalogue of 1775.[9]

Description (State 2)

All the examples of the plan which have been seen have the imprint beneath the bottom margin *Printed for T. Bowles in S[t] Pauls Church Y[d] John Bowles [ ] at the Black Horse in Cornhill and Rob[t]. Sayer at the Golden Buck in Fleet Street.* The words '*and son*' have been deleted.[10]

1. Stephen p. 206 (1727), with illustration. BL *Maps 4350.(4.); Bod Gough Maps Norfolk 10; Nfk.Lib.; Castle; RCF.
2. For Charles Viscount Townshend see Kirkpatrick (Prospect) [22], note 4. Corbridge incorrectly refers to him in the dedication not as Viscount Townshend but as Baron Lynn of Lynn Regis; Viscount Townshend's son sat in the House of Lords as Lord Lynn.
3. James Corbridge was almost certainly a native of the north of England, and we first hear of him in Newcastle-upon-Tyne in 1723, when he announced through the *Newcastle Weekly Courant* that he was proposing to produce a plan of that city. The outcome was the publication of the first professional survey of Newcastle, which was in very similar form, with drawings of churches and houses, to that which he subsequently produced in Norwich. Entries in newspapers both in Newcastle and in Norwich indicate that Corbridge came from Newcastle to Norfolk, probably initially to Great Yarmouth, during 1724. The Newcastle plan was not finally delivered to his subscribers there until early 1725, by which time Corbridge had been working on his prospect and plan of Great Yarmouth, delivered in July 1725. In the *Newcastle Weekly Courant* of 30 January 1724/25 Corbridge referred to the delivery of the Newcastle plan in Newcastle, but at the same time said that thee was an opportunity to subscribe for the plans of Great Yarmouth and Norwich 'now engraving'.
4. John Harris was a leading London engraver. Among other works were the first of the Buck prospects in the north of England, and also, for Corbridge, his plan of Newcastle and prospect of Great Yarmouth.
5. The *Norwich Mercury* of 2 December 1727, when Corbridge announced that the plan was 'ready to be delivered at the Lower Half Moon in the market Place, and by W. Chase in the Cockey lane who hath some to dispose of at 5/- each'.
6. The plan of Newcastle-upon-Tyne is extremely rare, and was not subsequently reprinted; BL Maps K.Top.32.(51.); Bod Gough Maps Northumberland 10.
7. Cleer's plan has been to a limited extent updated: the Duke of Norfolk's Palace which was demolished in 1711 is shown as a site, and no longer as a building; St. Andrew's Hall, 'New Hall', is now called 'The Exchange', and its octagon tower which had collapsed in 1712 is correctly no longer shown; 'Bethlem', the Bethel Hospital in Bethel Street (then Committee Street, and formerly Over Newport) founded in 1724, appears on a plan for the first time.
8. Happily most of the churches remain. Most of the houses featured have either disappeared, or have become so altered as to longer be recognisable; an exception is that of Mr. James Reeve, whose house still stands on the corner of Princes Street and Elm Hill.
9. The entry in Sayer & Bennetts' Catalogue of 1775 reads 'A Map of the City of Norwich, from an actual Survey, ornamented with the Elevations of the public and remarkable Buildings in and about the said City. By James Corbridge. On two sheets of Imperial Paper. Price 3/-'.
10. John Bowles' son Carington left his father's business in 1766, and it seems therefore that the plan was reprinted before 1766 with the reference to the son included, but that when he left the business the reference was removed.

[27] JAMES CORBRIDGE (Prospect)	**London**	**1730**

The NORTH EAST Prospect of NORWICH[1]   105 x 290 mm.

Source

In the bottom right corner panel of a map of the county of Norfolk (780 m 1140 mm.), a separate publication, described in the title as *This ACTUAL SURVEY of the COUNTY of NORFOLK,* by James Corbridge,[2] dated 1730, and with the imprint *E.Bowen Sculp.*[3] This is the first large scale map of the county, and contains prospects of Great Yarmouth, King's Lynn, and of Norwich.

Description.
The prospect of Norwich is a smaller version of that of Kirkpatrick [22], from which it has been directly copied. Corbridge has removed the large windmill, and people and animals in the foreground, and he has included a key to the Cathedral and the city's 35 churches, but other buildings such as the castle are not separately identified.

Later History
As is the case with Corbridge's plan [26] it seems that very few copies of the map in its original state have survived.[4] Apart from the map in the Bodleian, which could perhaps be a proof, all copies of the map seen by the author have the same imprint as the plan, *Printed for T.Bowles in S[t]. Pauls Church, and John Bowles,[ ] at the Black Horse in Cornhill, & Rob[t]. Sayer, at the Golden Buck in Fleet Street.* Again the words deleted are '*and son*'. Although the map continued to be advertised for sale by London booksellers, as late as 1795 in Bowles and Carver's Catalogue of that year, no copies have been seen with any later or corrected imprint.

1. Stephen refers to this prospect on p. 212 under the date 1750; Stephen incorrectly suggests that the plan is copied from Goddard and Chase [28], whereas it was Goddard and Chase who copied from Corbridge. Entries by both Stephen and Chubb in relation to Corbridge are in need of revision. Bod Gough Maps Norfolk 15; Nfk.Lib.; RCF.
2. For James Corbridge see notes on his plan, [26]. Corbridge's manuscript draft of the map (which does not include the Prospect) is in the Norfolk Record Office (NRO BL 72).
3. Emanuel Bowen, c.1693-1767, one of the leading 18th century engravers, and map and printsellers in London.
4. The only example of the plan without the later imprint known to the author is that in the Bodleian mentioned above, Bod (E) C17: 45 (22); it is printed on vellum, and there are a number of detailed differences between this map, (but not the Prospect), and the later edition.

[28]   THOMAS GODDARD AND WILLIAM CHASE   Norwich   1731

The NORTH EAST Prospect of NORWICH[1]   90 x 285 mm.

Source
A panel in the bottom left corner of a map of the county of Norfolk (600 x 1000 mm.) with the title *A New and Accurate Map of the county of Norfolk. Sold by T.Goddard and W. Chase, Booksellers in Norwich , 1731.*[2]

Origin of the Prospect
The map is a pirated copy of the map of the county by James Corbridge, with a similar layout of prospects, and side panels with details of parishes.[3] The Norwich Prospect is an almost exact copy of that of Corbridge [27], based on Kirkpatrick [22].

Description
The same view of the city from the North East as that of Corbridge. The title is in a scroll, top left; top right are the references, the same as Corbridge's, to the cathedral and 35 other churches. The map has been clearly engraved, but the name of the engraver is not known; it can

be contrasted with the rather heavier appearance of the almost identical map of Goddard and Goodman **[30]**.

Later History

The map was originally published in Norwich, and was reissued, dated **1745**, still with the names of Goddard and Chase. The plates were subsequently acquired by London mapsellers, and the map is found with a London imprint of **c.1775** *Printed for Carington Bowles No.69 St. Paul's Church Yard, and R. Sayer and I. Bennet in Fleet Street.*[4] No changes were made to the Norwich Prospect.

1. Stephen p. 208 (1731); the entries in Stephen and in Chubb in relation to this map are in need of revision. BL Maps K.Top.31.21.2 TAB; Bod G.A.Norf 80 220 (1); Nfk.Lib.; Castle.
2. For William Chase see Norwich Mercury, **[25]** note 2. Thomas Goddard (admitted freeman 1698, d.1751) was a leading Norwich bookseller, to whom William Chase had been apprenticed. Goddard was one of the early Norwich newspaper proprietors, having established the *Norwich Post-man* in January 1707, with Chase as his assistant. Chase took over Goddard's printing activities, but the two appear to have remained on friendly terms, advertising joint catalogue book sales.
3. Goddard and Chase were assisted by the Norwich city librarian and historian Benjamin Mackerell in producing a pirated version of Corbridge's map, which was advertised for sale in Chase's *Norwich Mercury*. For the dispute see David Stoker, *An Eighteenth Century Map Piracy*, in Norfolk Archaeology, Vol. 37, 1980, p. 123.
4. This map is wrongly described by Stephen p. 214 (1775) and by Chubb, p. 64 (1775), as being by Goddard and Goodman.

[29] GEORGE FOSTER   **London**   **1739**

The NORTH EAST PROSPECT of NORWICH[1]   72 x 120 mm.

Source

On a separately published map of the county of Norfolk (525 x 425 mm.), entitled *A New MAP of the County of NORFOLK done from the latest and best Observations*. The map is stated to be *Publish'd according to Act of Parliament Novr 16 1739. Printed for and sold by Geo: Foster at the White Horse in S^t. Pauls Church Yard London,*[2] and has the imprint *Roades Sculp^t.*[3]

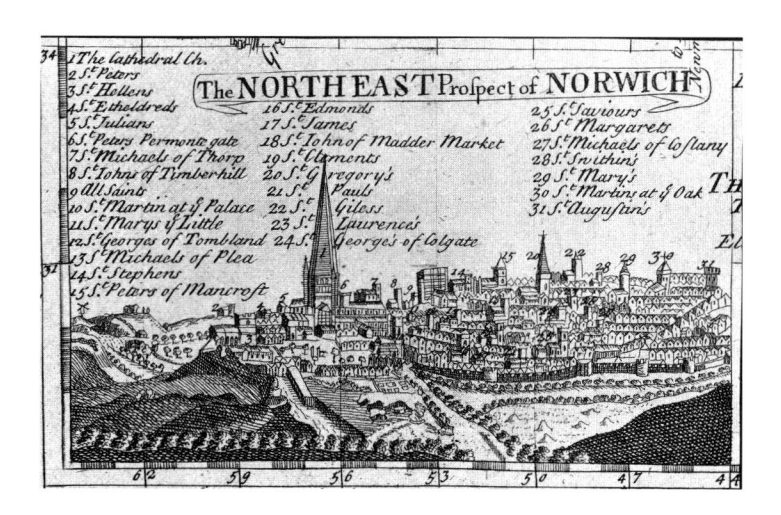

[29] 1739 George Foster

Description

The map appears to have been based on Goddard and Chase **[28]** but is very curiously distorted, in that the distance from north to south is about one and a half times that of the distance from west to east. The Prospect of the city is towards the bottom left of the map. Like the map, the Prospect seems to have been based on that of Goddard and Chase, ultimately derived from Kirkpatrick [22], but it gives a very inadequate and distorted view of the city. The city wall is prominent in the foreground, but much of the detail within the walls is poorly drawn, while the spire of the cathedral is greatly out of proportion to the cathedral itself, and to the city as a whole.

Later History

Notwithstanding that the map must be regarded as a curiosity in Norfolk maps, and unique amongst county mapping, it was republished in **1752** by George Foster's widow Elizabeth Foster, and again in **c.1761** by Robert Sayer. The later editions have revised imprints, but there are no changes to the Norwich Prospect.

1. Stephen p. 209 (1740). The entries in Stephen and in Chubb in relation to this map are in need of revision. BL Maps 4315 (37); Bod Gough Maps Norfolk 22; CUL Maps aa.77.75.1; Nfk.Lib.; Castle; NRO.
2. George Foster, London printer, publisher and mapseller, at premises where, according to his map, ' all County Chapmen may be furnished with variety of Maps and Prints Wholesale and Retale'. His map publications include a fine map of England and Wales in 1737 (Shirley, *British Isles*, 1988, p. 59) and a large scale plan of London in 1738,(Darlington and Hougego, *Maps of London,* p.89). His business was continued after his death by his widow Elizabeth Foster.
3. William Roades was also the engraver of the map and Norwich Prospect of Goddard and Goodman [30]. Other cartographic work included *A Pocket Map of the Cities of London and Westminster* published in 1731, Darlington and Howgego, op.cit. p. 86.

[30] THOMAS GODDARD and ROBERT GOODMAN   Norwich   1740

The NORTH EAST Prospect of NORWICH[1]   90 x 280 mm.

Source

The Prospect forms the panel in the bottom left corner of a separately produced map of the county of Norfolk (1025 x 590 mm.) entitled *A New and Accurate MAP of the County of NORFOLK Sold by Tho:Goddard and Robt Goodman Booksellers in Norwich.*[2] Outside the border of the map bottom right is the imprint of the engraver *Will[m]. Roades Sculp[t]*.

Description

The map, including the Norwich Prospect, is a very close copy of the map of Goddard and Chase [28]. There are differences in the title, and minor differences in certain names, but the two can best be distinguished by the inclusion on Goddard and Goodman's map of the name of the engraver, and the rather finer engraving of the map of Goddard and Chase. There is no noticeable difference between the two Prospects.

Later History

The map was reissued in **1757**, following Goddard's death, with the imprint *Sold by J. Dixon, C. Berry, R. Goodman and W. Wardlaw, Booksellers in Norwich.*[3] The plates were subsequently acquired by the London map and bookseller Robert Sayer who reissued the map in his name in c.**1760**; it continued to be advertised in sale catalogues, and eventually Sayer's successors in business, Laurie and Whittle, produced yet a further and final issue in **1797**.

1. Stephen p. 209 (1740), p. 212 (1757), and p. 216 (1797). The entry of Stephen at p. 214 (1775) is incorrect; the 1775 map and Prospect are those of Goddard and Chase [28]. BL *Maps 4315.(30.); Bod Gough Maps

Norfolk17; Nfk.Lib.; Castle; RCF.
2. Robert Goodman, Norwich bookseller from c.1734 to 1760, first near the Falcon, Duke's Palace, and later at the Upper Walk, Market Place; his stock was acquired by John Crouse, a leading Norwich printer and bookseller until his death in 1796.
3 J. Dixon was successor to the business of Thomas Goddard; Christopher Berry had taken over the shop at 13 Dove Lane of James Carlos, and he and his family continued as booksellers and stationers during the remainder of the century; William Wardlaw, in business from c. 1750, ran a large circulating library from 42, Market Place.

[31]   SAMUEL AND NATHANIEL BUCK   London   1741

THE NORTH-EAST PROSPECT OF THE CITY OF NORWICH[1]   300 x 795 mm.

Source
Initially a separate publication, with the imprint *Saml. And Nathl Buck delin et Sculp. Publish'd according to Act of Parliament Jany. 7th 1741. Garden Court N°. 1 Middle Temple, London.* The Prospect was subsequently issued in collections of engravings of castles, abbeys and towns which were published by the Bucks from 1726 to 1752.

Origin of the Prospect
Samuel Buck[2] began drawing and engraving views of buildings in Yorkshire in 1719. In c.1720, with the encouragement of the Society of Antiquaries, he began working on topographical views, and in c.1724 he was joined by his younger brother Nathaniel. In the years following they produced over 400 engravings of monasteries, abbeys, castles and other ruins, and a number of series of views of English and Welsh towns. They regularly toured the country, and were in East Anglia in 1737; following their visit they published, in 1741, Prospects of Yarmouth, King's Lynn, Bury St. Edmunds, Ipswich, and Colchester, as well as the two Prospects of Norwich.

Description (State 1)
A fine panoramic view of the city taken from a position very close to that of Kirkpatrick [22], with substantially the same content. Whether or not the Bucks were familiar with the earlier Prospect, theirs is clearly an original work, with considerable variation in the detail. In the foreground is a group of ladies and gentlemen admiring the view; the windmill which is such a prominent feature of Kirkpatrick's Prospect is missing. Above the top border is the title; below the bottom border are, to the left, the city arms, followed by eleven lines of text describing the city. Bottom right is a numbered key to churches and features shown on the Prospect, ending with 51, 'The hill where this drawing was taken'.

Later History
The plates of the Prospects were acquired br Robert Sayer in 1774. They were issued in that year with other Buck engravings, in three volumes with the title *BUCK'S ANTIQUITIES; OR VENERABLE REMAINS OF ABOVE 400 CASTLES, MONASTERIES, PALACES, ETC., ETC., IN ENGLAND and WALES. With near ONE HUNDRED VIEWS of CITIES AND CHIEF TOWNS.* The town Prospects are in Volume III, those of Norwich being numbered 53 and 54. The plates were subsequently reissued by Sayer and Bennett in **1775**, Sayer again in **1786**, Laurie and Whittle in **1795**, and finally by Whittle and Laurie as late as **1831**.[3]

Description (State 2)
The plate mark number 53 was added by Sayer outside the border top right. No other changes were made to the plate, or to the Bucks' original imprint.

[32] 1741 Samuel and Nathaniel Buck - The South-East Prospect of the City of Norwich

1. Stephen p. 209 (1741). BL Maps K.Top.31.34.b; BL Add. MS 23037.*f*.55; Bod Gough Maps 24; Bod Gough Maps Norfolk 13 (Proof); Nfk.Lib.; Castle; RCF.
2. Samuel Buck, 1696-1779. See Ralph Hyde, *A Prospect of Britain; the town panoramas of Samuel and Nathaniel Buck,* London , 1994.
3. In Sayer and Bennett's Catalogue for 1775 the three volumes were advertised at 18 guineas in sheets, or at 20 guineas 'elegantly bound'.
3. A number of reduced copies of the Bucks' Prospects were published during the 18th century and later. For the North-East Prospect see Armstrong [42]. Lithographic copies of both Prospects were produced by Jarrold and Sons, Norwich and were published by the firm of E.Bonser & Son, Tea Merchants and Tasters, of 10 The Walk, Norwich, and 87 Tower Hill, London in c.1885, under the title of *Prospects of the City of Norwich in 1743* (sic).

[32] SAMUEL AND NATHANIEL BUCK　　　　　London　　　　　1741

THE SOUTH-EAST PROSPECT OF THE CITY OF NORWICH[1]　　　300 x 795 mm.

Source
The same as the North-East Prospect [31], with the same imprint.

Description (State 1)
A companion to the North-East Prospect, the city viewed from the hill above the river opposite Pull's Ferry. At the foot of the hill, on which a number of people are enjoying the countryside and the view, is the river itself, with numerous boats of various kinds. In the foreground across the river is the Cathedral Close, with the canal from the ferry towards the cathedral very prominently shown, and the sweep of the river running southwards towards the warehouse buildings off King Street. The view is such that the layout of the city beyond the cathedral and the castle is not as apparent as in the case of the North-East Prospect, but the city wall and the gates on the south and south west of the city are clearly shown,

Later History
The same as that of the North-East Prospect.[2]

Description (State 2)
The plate mark 54 has been added outside the border, top right.

1. Stephen p. 210 (1741). BL Maps K.Top.31.34.c.; BL Add. MS 23037.*f*.55; Bod Gough Maps 24; Bod Gough Maps Norfolk 13 (Proof); Nfk.Lib.; Castle; RCF.
2. For reduced versions of the South-East Prospect see Hinton [34], Ryland [35], Goadby [40] and the Political Magazine [45]. Nfk.Lib. has two copies of another rather poorly drawn reduced version (105 x 290 mm.) with a single line border, and below the bottom border the title *THE SOUTH-EAST PROSPECT OF THE CITY OF NORWICH.* There are 50 numbered references, after Buck, on the Prospect, but without a key. The source of this Prospect has not been established.

[33]　FRANCIS BLOMEFIELD　(1)　　　　　Norwich　　　　　1746

A PLAN of the CITY of NORWICH[1]　　　　　670 x 585 mm.
　　　　　　　　　　　　　　　　　　(With side borders added 820 x 585 mm.)
A Scale of 400 yards = 4"　(102 mm.)　　1:3600　　17.6" = 1 mile

Source
The plan was produced with the intention that it should be issued with Volume II of Francis

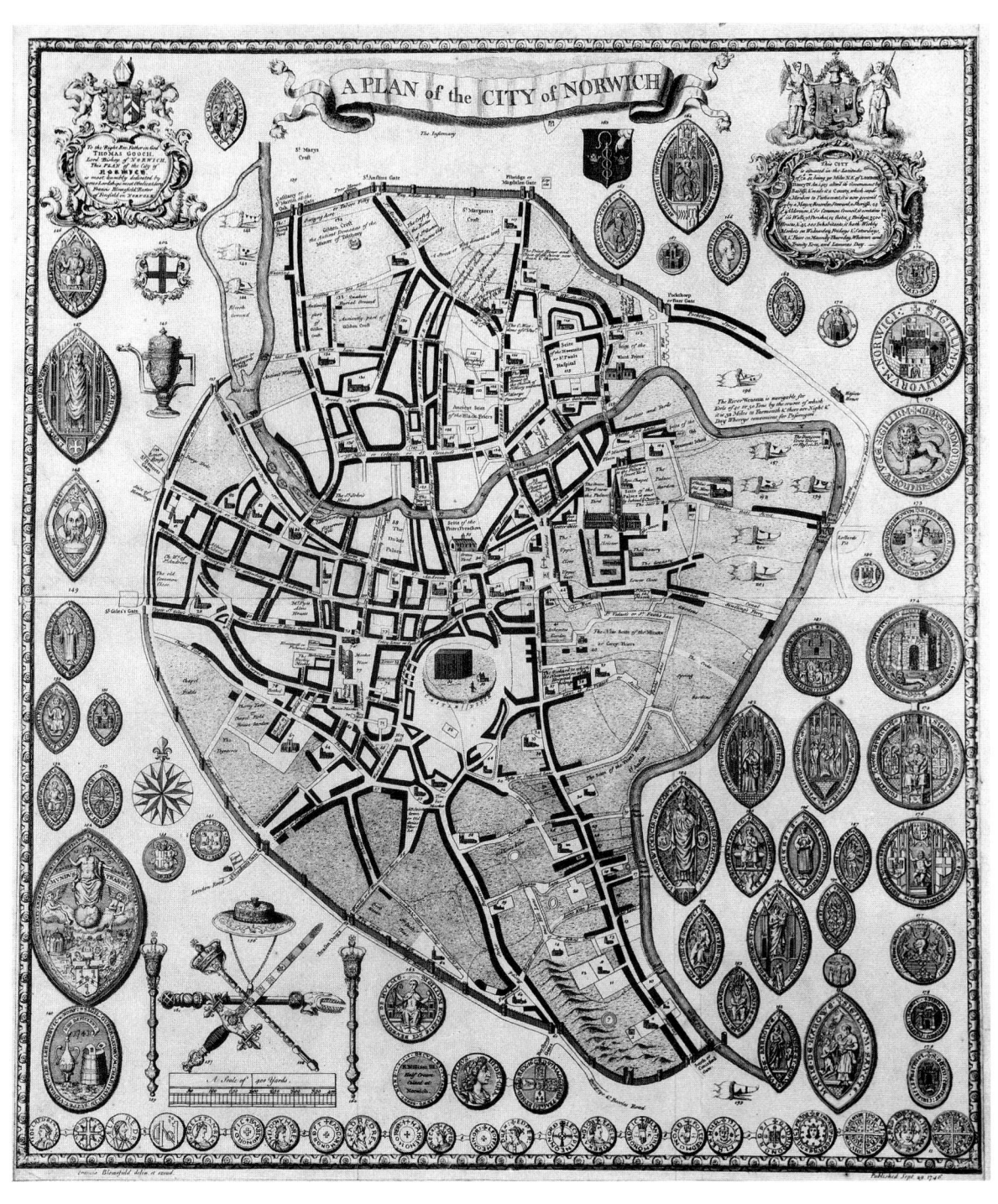

[33] 1746 Francis Blomefield

Blomefield's *AN ESSAY Towards a TOPOGRAPHICAL HISTORY of the COUNTY of NORFOLK*.[2] After the completion of Volume I and its printing in Fersfield in 1739, Blomefield proceeded with Volume II, which was devoted entirely to Norwich. The final part was dated 31 May 1745, and the Volume, subtitled as *CONTAINING The HISTORY of The CITY of NORWICH*, was printed in Norwich, and dated 1745. However when Volume II was printed the plan of the city had not been completed,[3] and it was not until January of the following year 1746/7 that the plan was available for subscribers. It was finally issued at the same time as the first part of Volume III of the *History* (which in the event Blomefield was destined not to complete personally), and the plan was also available for sale separately.[4] It is shown, outside the border bottom right, as *Published Sept. 29.1746*.

Blomefield had meanwhile also decided to offer the Norwich parts of the *History* as a separate Norwich volume, with the title of *THE HISTORY OF THE CITY AND COUNTY OF NORWICH*; the same pages were used, and the contents were exactly the same, issued with a different title page and binding. Notwithstanding that the text was not completed until 1745, the title page had been produced in advance, is dated 1741, and was shown as having been printed at Fersfield.

Origin of the Plan
Beneath the plan is the imprint *Francis Blomefield delin. and excud.*, and Blomefield was clearly personally concerned with the drawing of the plan.[2] However he had complained from time to time about finding local engravers for the illustrations in the *History*, and for the engraving of the plan he employed a leading London engraver, George Vertue.[5]

Description
The plan, which has an ornamental border, is similar in general appearance to those of Cleer **[16 and 17]** and of Corbridge **[26]**. However the importance of Blomefield's plan is in the very substantial amount of extra detail which is contained in the many references, and in the numerous engravings surrounding the plan itself. The references were printed separately in two panels, included in the book, but also sold separately with the plan, so designed with matching borders that they could be added to the sides of the plan. The cathedral, churches, the castle and other principal buildings are shown in profile; a feature is the naming of all the roads, but earlier or alternative names are added; for the first time an attempt has been made to show parish boundaries by dotted lines. The title is in a scroll top centre. On the left is the dedication to Blomefield's bishop, Thomas Gooch, with the arms of the bishopric. Around the plan are the arms of the deanery, and of the city, the civic regalia and plate, numerous seals, coins and swan marks. On the left of the plan is a compass indicator, and, bottom left, the scale.

Later History
Blomefield died in 1752. Volumes I and II of the History had been completed, but part only of Volume III. The full story of the eventual completion of the work by the Reverend Charles Parkin is beyond the scope of this note. Suffice it to say that Parkin completed Volume III, and Volumes IV and V, by about 1763, but did not live to see them published. The manuscripts were eventually sold to and published by the King's Lynn bookseller William Whitttingham. The Norwich volume, with the plan, was published as *The History and Antiquities of the City of Norwich in the County of Norfolk* under the name of Charles Parkin by Whittingham in King's Lynn in **1783**. A new edition of the whole of the *History*, with a new plan **[47]**, was published in eleven volumes in 1806.

1. Stephen p. 210 (1746). BL G.3786-90; Maps K.Top.31.31; Bod Gough Maps Norfolk 18; Nfk.Lib.; Castle; RCF.

2. Francis Blomefield, 1705-1752, rector of Fersfield in Norfolk from 1730 until his early death from smallpox. He began to publish his monumental work on the history of the county in parts, the first part of Volume I being issued in March 1736. Volume I was completed and printed in his village of Fersfield in 1739, but in between March 1743 and August 1745 he moved his printing press to Willow Lane in Norwich.

3. In a letter dated 10 March 1745/6 to William Cole at King's College, Cambridge, Blomefield says 'My map is now near finished, Mr Vertue hath the 2d revise. I will get a 1st. no. of next volume fit to deliver together': *The Correspondence of the Reverend Francis Blomefield (1705-1752)*, Norfolk Record Society, Volume LV, 1992, p. 242, and generally the Introduction by David Stoker.

4. From a letter from Blomefield dated 14 January 1746/7- 'I have at last published my first number of my third volume of my History of Norfolk, and also the plan of Norwich to be prefixed to the 2nd vol., it needs no references, they being in the book; but for such as have not the book, or choose it as a picture, I have added references & doubled the price, those for the vols only being 2s 6d & those for the pictures , 5s.': *The Correspondence,* op.cit., p. 243.

5. George Vertue, 1684-1756, a prominent London antiquary and engraver, and member of the Society of Antiquaries.

[34]   JOHN HINTON   London   1753

The South-East Prospect of the CITY of NORWICH.[1]   145 x 290 mm.

Source
From Volume XIII of the *Universal Magazine of Knowledge and Pleasure,*[2] published by John Hinton[3] in November 1753. Also in this volume is a map of Norfolk engraved by Emanuel Bowen,[4] and six pages of text containing a short history of the county.

Description
Above the top border is the imprint *Engrav'd for the Universal Magazine, for J. Hinton at the King's Arms in Newgate Street.* The Prospect is a reduced version of the Bucks' South-East Prospect **[32]**. The figures in the foreground have been changed, but in all other respects the Prospect closely follows the original on which it is based. The border consists of a thicker outer and a thinner inner line; the title is below the bottom border. Churches and other buildings and features are numbered from 1 to 43, the references being found in the accompanying text.

Later History
The Prospect is included as a frontispiece to *THE HISTORY AND ANTIQUITIES OF THE CITY OF NORWICH....Collected....By the late Rev. Charles Parkin, A. M. Rector of Oxburgh.*[5] *Lynn. Printed by W. Whittingham; for J. Robson Book-seller, New-Bond Street; W. Lane, Leadenhall-Street London. MDCCLXXXIII.*[6] The imprint above the top border referring to the *Universal Magazine* has been deleted, but otherwise the Prospect and the title are unchanged. The references to the churches and other features are given on page 312 of the book.

1. Not in Stephen. BL P.P. 5439; Nfk.Lib.; RCF.
2. From its first issue in June 1747 the *Universal Magazine* included pages about individual counties. County maps appeared at irregular intervals between 1747 and 1766, and were engraved either by Emanuel Bowen, Thomas Kitchin, or Richard William Seale. Hinton published the *Universal Magazine* until his death in 1781; further issues continued at intervals until 1799.
3. John Hinton, London bookseller and publisher. He was also the initial publisher of the *Large English Atlas* in 1749.
4. Chubb, p. 53 (1753); another different map of the county was published by the *Universal Magazine* in August 1793, Chubb, p. 76 (1793).
5. Although this work is ascribed to the late Charles Parkin, it is based on the Norwich section of Blomefield's *History of Norfolk* ; see Blomefield's plan of 1746, **[33]**. This seems to have been a speculative venture by the

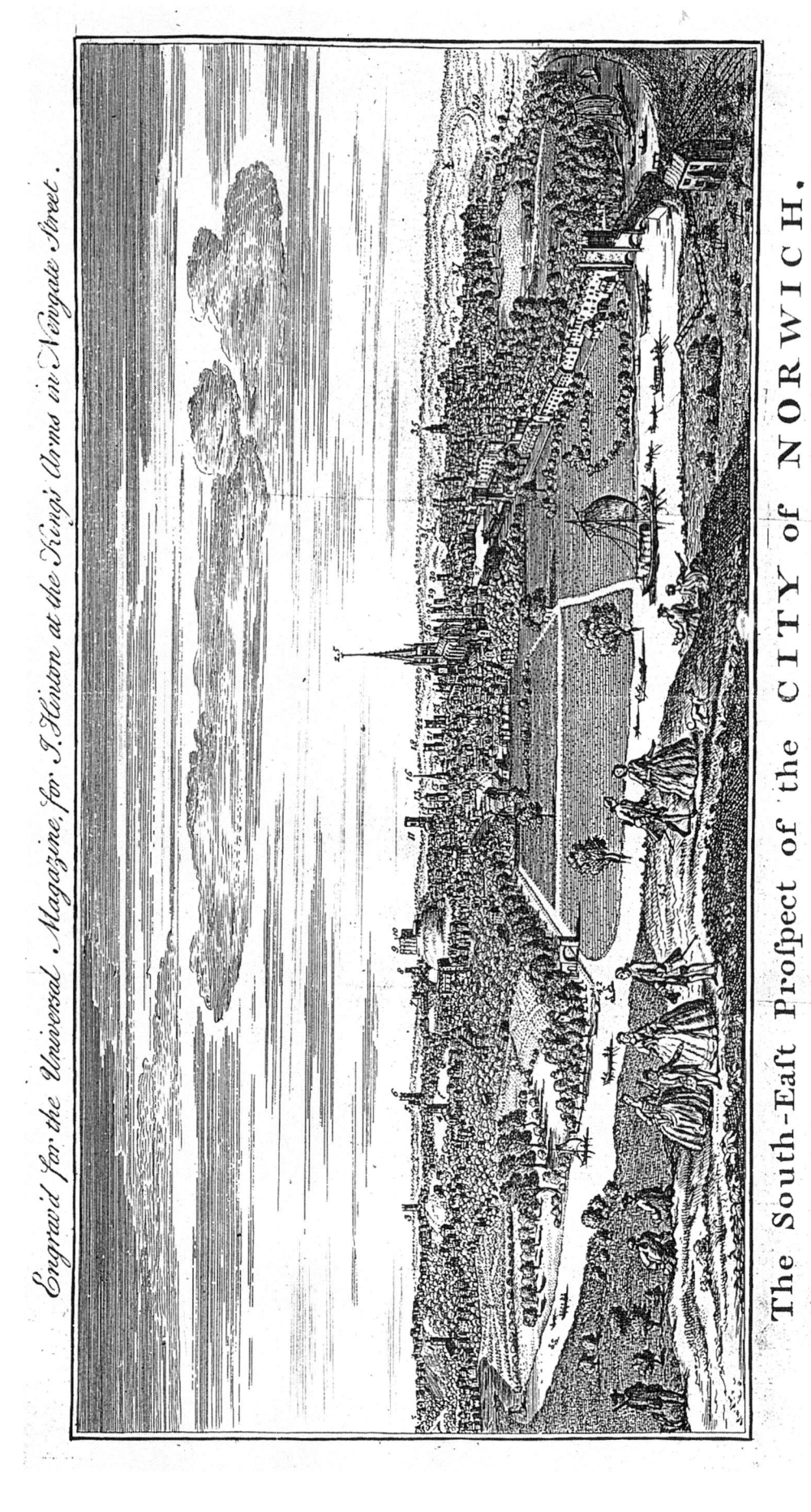

[34] 1753 John Hinton - The South-East Prospect of the City of Norwich

King's Lynn printers, W. Whittingham, with the London booksellers, Robson. The plan of Norwich which appeared in the reprint of the Norwich volume of Blomefield's *History* was not included in this work.
6. Stephen p. 215 (1783). BL 290.f.36; Nch.Lib.

[35] JOHN RYLAND London 1764

The South East View of Norwich[1] 100 x 176 mm.

Source
The View or Prospect is contained in the second volume of a work entitled *England Illustrated, or a Compendium of the Natural History, Geography, Topography, and Antiquities Ecclesiastical and Civil, of England and Wales. With maps of the several counties, and engravings of many Remains of Antiquity, remarkable buildings and principal Towns. In two volumes. London: Printed for R. and J. Dodsley,*[2] *in Pall Mall, MDCCLXIV.* It is found within a section of the work, pages 90 - 113, containing a short description of the county of Norfolk, and follows page 90. The back is plain.

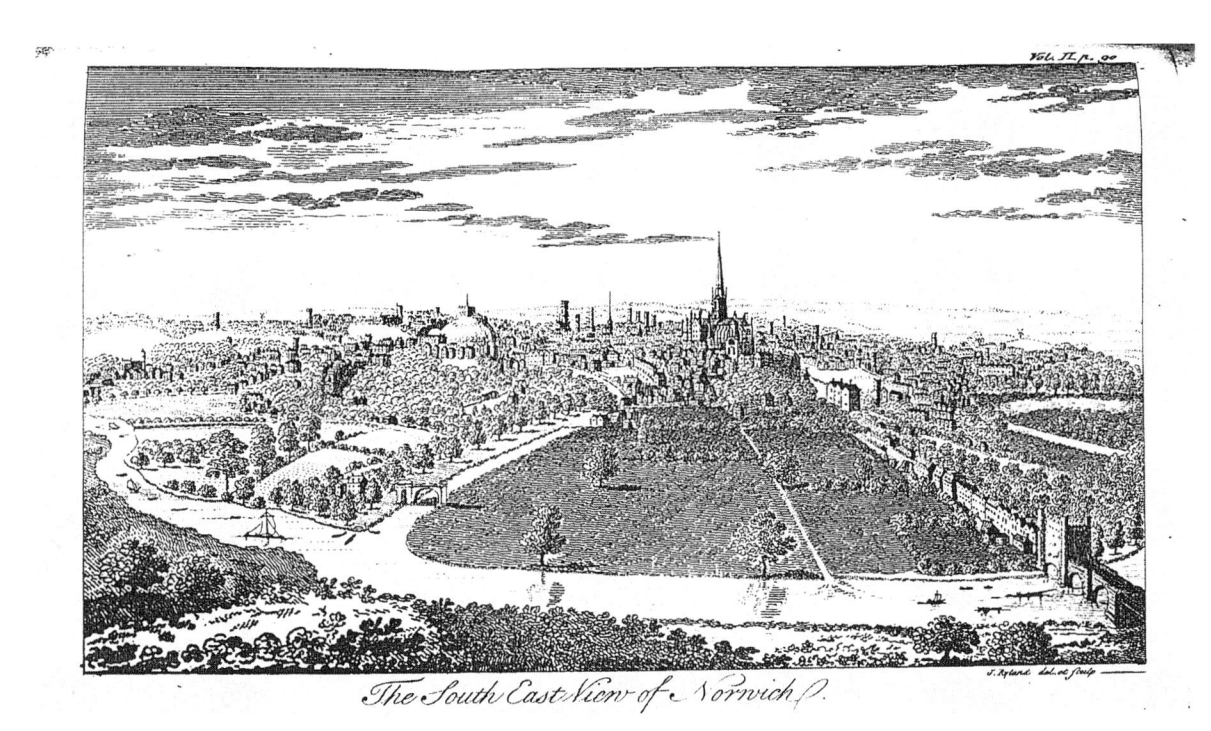

[35] 1764 John Ryland

Description
The View is a smaller version of the Bucks' South-East Prospect of the city **[32]**, from which it has been copied. There are no figures in the foreground, and fewer boats on the river, but the cathedral, the castle, the river, the Lower Close, Bishopgate and Bishop Bridge are prominent and unmistakable features. The border is a single line. Above the border, top right, is the direction to the binder, *Vol.II p.90*; below the bottom border is the title, and outside the border, bottom right, is the imprint *J. Ryland del. et sculp—*[3]

1. Not in Stephen. BL 190.b.8-9; Bod GA Gen Top 42.184-85.
2. Robert Dodsley, 1703-1764, publisher, and also writer, poet and dramatist, in partnership with his brother James, 1724-1797. For a detailed description of *England Illustrated* see Hodson, *County Atlases*, 1997, p.165.
3. John Ryland, engraver, of Ryland & Bryer, engravers and printsellers at the King's Arms, Cornhill, and later at the Old Bailey, London. His work included the 1766 issue of Kirby's map of Suffolk, and a map of Turnpike Roads in 1767. Ryland himself seems to have had a somewhat chequered career, having become bankrupt in 1776, and again in 1789.

[36] SAMUEL KING (1)   Norwich and London   1766

A New Plan of the City of Norwich[1]   955 x 750 mm.

Scale of 22 Chains 22 Yards in each = 6.562" (167 mm.)   1:2652   23.89" = 1 mile

Source
A separate publication, with the title top centre below the border as above, and an additional title *THE CITY AND COUNTY OF NORWICH* in a decorated border bottom left. There is a lengthy dedication to the mayor, aldermen and council of the city by Samuel King Land Surveyor,[2] and following his signature *Subscrib'd for in the Mayoralty of Ja^s. Poole Esq.1766*.[3]   Below the bottom border is the imprint *Printed for and Sold by Saml. King Senr. near Charing Cross Norwich, and Saml. King Junr. at the Corner of Grange Court, in Clement's Lane, Clare Market, London.*

Origin of the Plan
In the *Norwich Mercury* of the 25 January 1766, Samuel King, Land Surveyor, advertised Proposals for printing by subscription a New and Accurate Plan of the City of Norwich taken from his actual survey; the price was 5s., 2/6d. on subscribing and 2/6d. on delivery, subscriptions to be taken by the author at his house, and he asked for help with names from ancient writings. The publication of the plan was announced in the *Norwich Mercury* of 26 July 1766, to be sold by King at his home near Charing Cross [Norwich], and also by the booksellers W.Chase, C.Berry, and W. Wardlow.[4]

Description
A fine detailed plan, with drawings of the cathedral, churches, the castle and other public buildings. Around the plan itself are drawings of the Guildhall, the New Chapel in S^t. George's,[5] the Assembly House, the South West Prospect of the Cathedral, and of the Castle. The city arms are top right; there is a compass indicator top centre, with on either side the arms of the bishopric and of the deanery. A feature of the plan is the inclusion of the names of the inns, and for the benefit of the mayor, in the position close to the later Foundry Bridge 'Vinegar Yard and Office erected by James Poole'.

Later History
It was recorded in the *Norfolk Chronicle* of 20 October 1773, that the stocks of King's plans of Norwich had been bought by Martin Booth, bookseller, in the Market Place, Norwich. They were offered at 2s.6d. for the large plan, and 1s. for the small plan.

1. Stephen p. 212 (1766). BL Maps K. Top 31.32.; Bod Gough Maps Norfolk 25; Nfk.Lib.; CUL Maps aa.77.76.1; Nfk.Lib.; Castle; RCF.
2. Samuel King was a professional surveyor based in Norwich, and he is known for producing estate, inclosure,

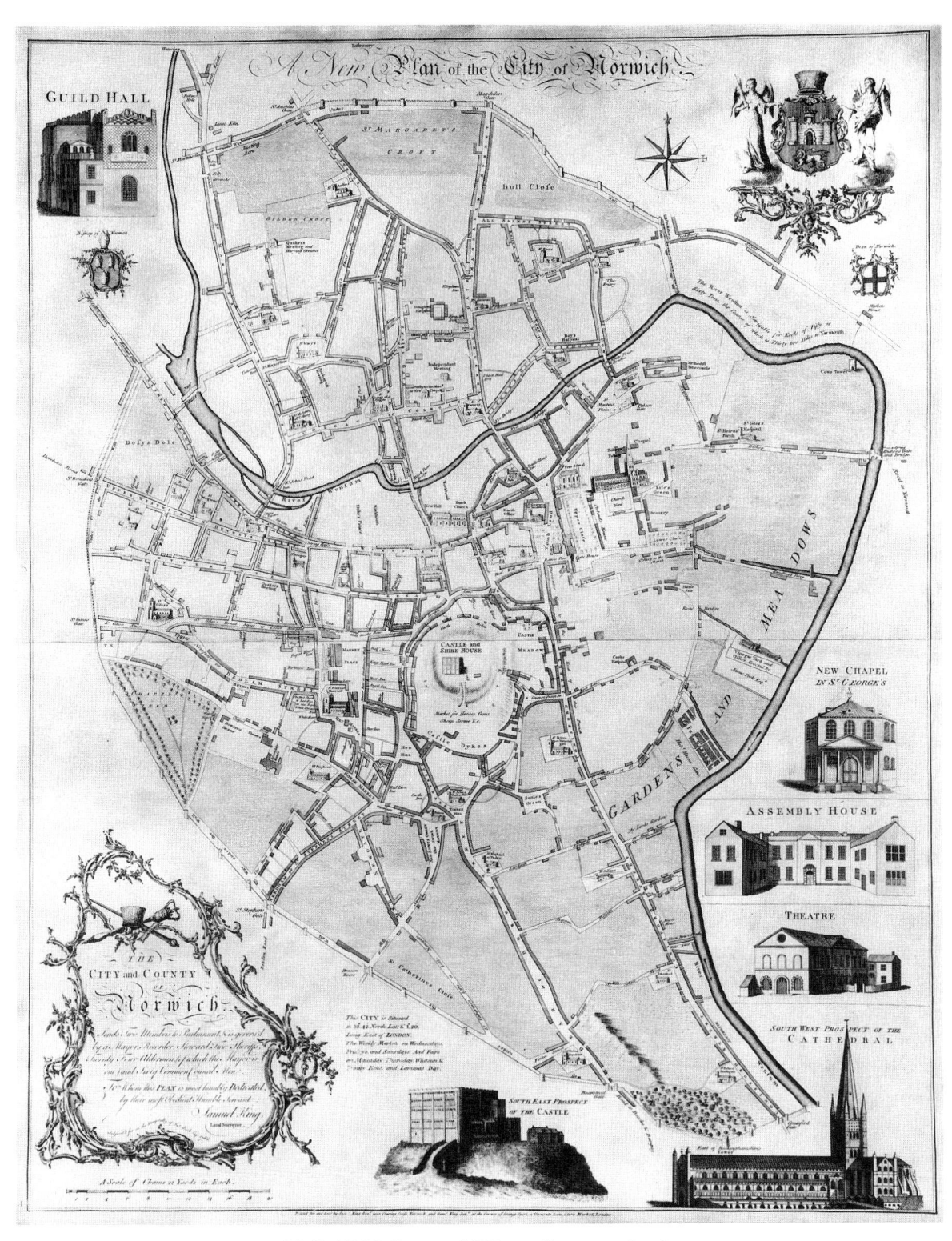

[36] 1766 Samuel King (larger plan)

and other maps and plans from 1763 onwards; his death was recorded in the *Norfolk Chronicle* of 17 July 1779, when he was described as 'Mr. King, Surveyor, son of the late Mr. King of this City'.

3. James Poole, grocer and wine merchant, sheriff in 1764 and mayor in 1765; he built a fine house at 3 Redwell Plain, which became Gurney's Bank House, demolished in 1927 for the construction of the new Barclay's Bank. He was made bankrupt in 1773, and died in January 1780.

4. For Chase see Norwich Mercury [25]; for Berry and Wardlow see Goddard and Goodman [30].

5. The Octagon Chapel, Colegate, built by Thomas Ivory, 1754-56 as a Presbyterian chapel, becoming Unitarian after 1820.

[37] SAMUEL KING   (2)   Norwich and London   1766

A NEW PLAN OF THE CITY OF NORWICH[1]   470 x 375 mm.

A Scale of 18 Chains = 3" (76 mm.)   1:4800   (13.2" = 1 mile)

Source

The plan was first produced and sold as a separate publication, shortly after the sale of Samuel King's larger plan [36]. The plan has the imprint of *Samuel King, Land Surveyor,*[2] *Publish'd in the Mayoralty of Jn°. Patteson Esq*[r].[3] *1766*, and has the same imprint below the bottom border as the larger plan, referring to the printing for and sale by the Kings, senior and junior, in Norwich and in London.

Description

The plan is a reduced version of the King's larger plan, with substantially the same content. The walls, churches, and some other buildings are shown in profile as on the larger plan, although with less detail, and the names of the inns are given. The border consists of two lines, the outer thicker than the inner. The title is beneath the border top centre, and around the actual plan of the city are drawings of the Guildhall, the arms of the bishopric, deanery and city, the New Chapel in St. Georges, Assembly House, Theatre, Cathedral and Castle. To the left of the plan are the usual 36 references to the churches; as with the larger plan there is a decorated panel, bottom left, containing the dedication and Samuel King's signature, and the reference to the date of publication.

Later History

King's smaller plan, together with the *NORTH-EAST PROSPECT* [38], were included as additional illustrations in most copies of *THE HISTORY OF THE CITY AND COUNTY OF NORWICH FROM THE EARLIEST ACCOUNTS TO THE PRESENT TIME* with the imprint *NORWICH: PRINTED BY JOHN CROUSE,*[4] *AND SOLD BY M. BOOTH, BOOKSELLER, IN THE MARKET-PLACE. M.DCC.LXVIII.*[5] The work is dedicated to the mayor, sheriffs, aldermen and common-council of the city by *The EDITOR* ; the name of the editor or author is not given, and has not been established. The *HISTORY* was divided into two Parts; Samuel King's plan is usually found at the front of Part II, but in some copies at the front of Part I; at the front of the other Part is usually found the *NORTH-EAST PROSPECT*.

As referred to in the note to King's large plan, the stock of plans was acquired by Martin Booth in 1773, the smaller plan then being offered for sale as a separate item for 1s.

1. Stephen p. 213 (1766). BL 290.c.34; Bod Gough Maps Norfolk 24; Nfk.Lib.; Castle; RCF.
2. For Samuel King see note 2 to his larger plan, [36].
3. John Patteson, 1727-1774, was sheriff in 1761 and mayor in 1766. His firm Patteson & Iselin carried on a considerable trading business at home and overseas. In 1765 he built the house in Surrey Street, the site of which

is shown although not named on the plan, subsequently the home of Sir Samuel Bignold, and now owned by the Norwich Union.

4. John Crouse was actively involved as a printer in Norwich from 1760, until his death in 1796. He acquired the stock of Robert Goodman (see [30]) in 1760 (*Norwich Mercury* 19 July 1760); in 1761 he printed a revised *Norwich Gazette*, which became the *Norfolk Chronicle* in 1769; he was in partnership with William Stevenson from 1785 to 1790, and with Stevenson and Jonathan Matchett until his death.

5. Martin Booth, a leading Norwich bookseller, and dealer in prints, paintings, maps, coins and medals. His 248 page catalogue of 1777 contained over 15,000 volumes. He died in 1783, the business continuing first as Booth & Son, and then as G. & T. Booth.

[38] MARTIN BOOTH   Norwich   1768

The NORTH-EAST PROSPECT of the CITY of NORWICH[1]   170 x 325 mm.

Source
The Prospect is found as a separate publication, and also as an illustration included in *THE HISTORY OF THE CITY AND COUNTY OF NORWICH FROM THE EARLIEST ACCOUNTS TO THE PRESENT TIME* with the imprint NORWICH: PRINTED BY JOHN CROUSE, AND SOLD BY M. BOOTH, BOOKSELLER, IN THE MARKET-PLACE. M.DCC.LXVIII [2]

Description
This is a much reduced version of Kirkpatrick's Prospect [22]. The origin is immediately obvious, and while certain features including the figures in the foreground have been removed, the large windmill on the right is retained. Subject to the exigencies of size the details of the city have been reproduced. The title is in a scroll above the view of the city. Beneath the bottom border are references to the 36 churches, with the city arms in the centre.[3]

1. Stephen p. 213 (1768). BL 290.c.33 ; Bod Gough Maps 25; Nfk.Lib.
2. For the inclusion of the Prospect in the *HISTORY* see the Later History of Samuel King's smaller plan [37], and notes 4 and 5 relating to John Crouse and Martin Booth. .
3. There is no indication as to the engraver, but Martin Booth was a printseller, and it seems likely that he will have commissioned it for sale. He offered it as a separate item for 6d. Some examples of the print have the number 19 outside the border, top right, which suggests that it may have been included in another publication; if so this has not been identified.

[39] CLUER DICEY   London   c.1768

The North-East Prospect of the CITY of NORWICH[1]   175 x 325 mm.

Source
The print appears to have been a separate publication.

Description
The Prospect is very obviously based on Kirkpatrick's North-East Prospect [22], and is very similar to the Martin Booth Prospect [38]. The plate is marginally different in size, and there are observable differences, particularly in the treatment of the clouds and sky. In the references, 33 is S[t]. Bennets and 36 S[t]. Austin's, instead of S[t]. Benedicts and S[t]. Augustines in [39]. Bottom right is the imprint *Sold by C. Dicey & Co. in Aldermary Church Yard* . Other examples of the Prospect do not have the Dicey imprint, but in other respects appear to be identical.

1. Stephen p. 214 (1768), without the Dicey imprint. Private collection.
2. The Diceys were a well known family of printers and mapsellers from c.1720; the form C. Dicey & Co. was adopted in 1756.

[40] ROBERT GOADBY   London   1776

The South East View of the City of Norwich[1]   115 x 190 mm.

Source

From *A NEW DISPLAY OF THE BEAUTIES OF ENGLAND. LONDON. Printed for R.GOADBY;*[2] *and sold by J.Towers, at No. 111, in Fore-Street, near Cripplegate; and by R.Baldwin, No.47, in Paternoster Row------M,DCC,LXXVI.* A short description of Norfolk is contained in pages 25 to 45 of Volume II, including Norwich at pages 26 to 28. The Norwich View is placed opposite p.26.

Description

This is another small prospect or view based on the Bucks' South-East Prospect of the city [32], without references. It is very similar to the the South East View of Ryland [35], and at first sight they might appear to be taken from the same plate. However close comparison reveals minor differences, and while the actual views of the city are virtually identical in size, this plate is slightly larger both in height and width, and consequently extent, than that of Ryland. The title is below the border, which is formed by a single line. Above the border, top right, is *V.II. P.26*.

Later History

Unchanged Second and Third editions of the work were published in 1776 and 1777. In **1787** appeared *A NEW EDITION, Revised and Enlarged.* This later edition was *Printed for R. GOADBY and Co. and sold by R. BALDWIN No.47, in Paternoster-row. M.DCC.LXXXVII.* The description of Norfolk is contained on pages 108 to 131 of Volume II. The Norwich View is placed opposite p.108, and above the top border, top left, is *Vol.II*, and, top right, *Pa.108*.[3]

This same View has been found in later publications. Reference is made is made to *The Beauties of England and Wales* in relation to the plan of the city by Cole [48]. The text relating to Norfolk (but without the plan by Cole) was published in Volume XI, with the title *THE BEAUTIES of ENGLAND AND WALES; or DELINEATIONS TOPOGRAPHICAL HISTORICAL AND DESCRIPTIVE Vol. XI . London, Publish'd by Vernor Hood & Sharpe, Poultry, Aug[t]. 1. 1809.* Although the Goadby View of Norwich was not originally included in this section of the work, copies to which it has been added have been seen, (Nch.Lib.). The Norfolk section was subsequently reprinted separately as *A TOPOGRAPHICAL AND HISTORICAL DESCRIPTION OF THE County of Norfolk, by John Britton, London, Printed for Sherwood, Neely and Jones....Successors to Vernor, Hood and Sharp,31, Poultry. 1813.* Again the View of Norwich appears not originally to have been included, but it has been added to a copy of the work in a private collection. In these examples the View has been unchanged, but in one instance the page reference above the border, top right, is now *V. 11. 1.20.*

1. Not in Stephen. BL 290.a.10.
2. Robert Goadby was in business in Sherborne, producing an illustrated bible in 1759, but appears to have sold his work in London. Other members of the Goadby family were publishers in London in the latter part of the 18th century, one Samuel Goadby, being one of the founder members of the S.P.C.K.
3. BL 577.f.12-13.; Bod G.A.Gen.top.8⁰ 368.

[41] JOHN THOMPSON   Norwich   1779

No Scale is shown

PLAN of the CITY of NORWICH[1]   415 x 315 mm.

Source
Produced for the ten volume *HISTORY AND ANTIQUITIES OF THE COUNTY OF NORFOLK. NORWICH: PRINTED BY J. CROUSE, FOR M. BOOTH, BOOKSELLER. M.DCC.LXXXI.*[2] The work, which was originally published in weekly numbers at 6d. each, is very largely based on Blomefield's *History* (see [33]). The author is not named, but the *History* is attributed to Mostyn John Armstrong, who was almost certainly responsible for the plan.[3] The plan follows the title page in Volume X of the *History*, which contains *The City and County of Norwich*; it has the imprint *Publish'd as the Act Directs, May 31, 1779. Engrav'd for the History of Norfolk by J. Thompson of Norwich.*[4]

Description
The plan closely follows the smaller plan of Samuel King [37]. It is very slightly smaller, but the details are almost identical, with the same references to the churches in the same order. Whereas King has drawn the walls, gates, churches and some other buildings in profile, Thompson has only shown the line of the walls, and the only building in profile is the castle. The border consists of a double line. Above the border is the title; top right are the arms of the bishopric and of the city. Centre right is a compass indicator, above drawings of the 'New Chapel in S^t. George's' (the Octagon Chapel), and of the Guildhall. Bottom left are the 36 'References' to the churches, and drawings of the Assembly House, and of the Theatre Royal. The imprint of the engraver is within the border, bottom right; below the bottom border is the dedication, which is *To The Right Worshipfull ROGER KERRISON, Esqr. Mayor, 1779.*[5]

1. Stephen p.214 (1779). BL 290.h.29; Bod Gough Maps Norfolk 23; Nfk.Lib.; Castle; RCF.
2. For J. Crouse and M. Booth see Samuel King's plan [37], notes 4 and 5.
3. Mostyn John Armstrong was a trained surveyor, initially working on a number of important mapping projects with his father Captain Andrew Armstrong. These included a large scale survey of Northumberland published in 1769, and a survey of Berkshire in 1771. They then moved to Scotland, Mostyn John himself producing a county survey of Peebles in 1775, followed by *An Actual Survey of the Great Post-Roads between London and Edinburgh* in 1776. At this point Mostyn John moved to Norwich, married, and was made a lieutenant in the Norfolk Militia. In the *Norwich Mercury* of 30 November 1776, he first mentions his intention to produce a new map of the county of Norfolk, although in the event, and this is a separate story about the mapping of the county, the map was never completed and published. In the meantime however Armstrong became involved with John Crouse's *HISTORY*. In the *Norfolk Chronicle* of 11 October 1777 Crouse announced that he was considering publishing a new and complete History of Norfolk; he asked anyone who had material to illustrate the work, or to correct any errors in Blomefield's *History,* to communicate with him, or with Mostyn John Armstrong.
Although Armstrong's name is not referred to in the text, a number of the illustrations carry his signature, and there seems little doubt that he masterminded the work, and that he was responsible for the plan of the city. That he had personally produced a plan, although this may not have been the same plan as engraved by Thompson, is confirmed by a report in the *Norwich Mercury* of 26 February 1780, that 'At a general assembly of the Corporation on Thursday last....Mr. M. J. Armstrong presented the Corporation with a very neat and accurate plan drawn by him of the County of the City of Norwich, which was ordered to be framed and glazed, and hung in the court room of the Guildhall.' In Chase's *Norwich Directory* of 1783, when he was living at 2 Red-Well Street in the city, he was described as County Surveyor. He died in 1791, and his will is in the NRO.
4. In *The Norwich Directory* of 1783 John Thompson is named as an engraver, living at no. 1, Gun Lane.
5. Roger Kerrison, mayor in 1778, and again in 1802, High Sheriff of the county in 1800, and knighted in that year. He was a banker, and receiver-general for taxes in Norfolk. Following his death in 1803 the government was unable to recover taxes which he had collected, and made his banking business, Roger Kerrison & Son, bankrupt.

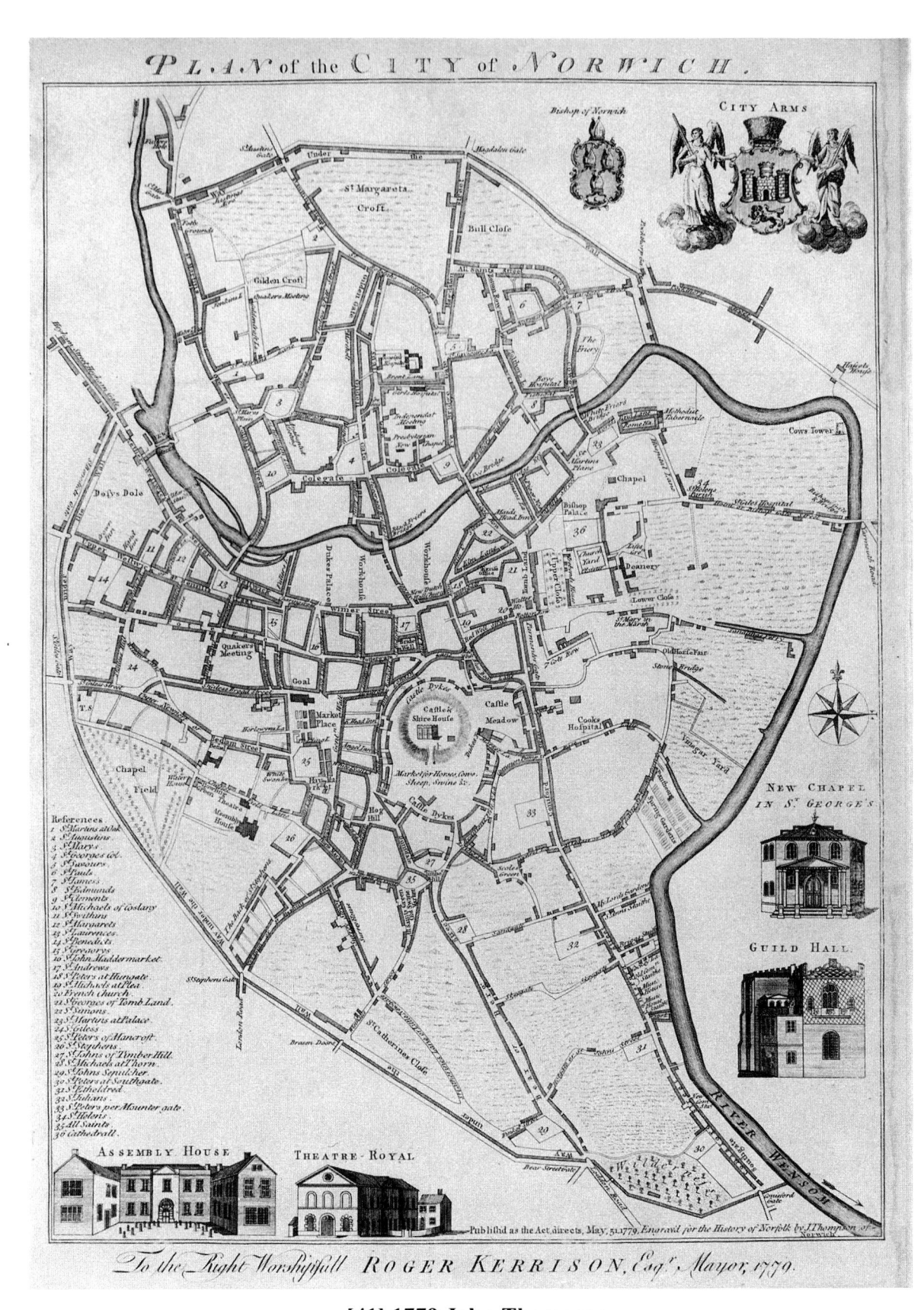

[41] 1779 John Thompson

[42]   MARCUS ARMSTRONG   Norwich   1781

NORTH EAST PROSPECT of the CITY OF NORWICH [1]   100 x 200 mm.

Source

From the same work as the plan of John Thompson [41]. The Prospect is placed before the title page of Volume X of the *HISTORY AND ANTIQUITIES OF THE COUNTY OF NORFOLK CONTAINING The City and County of Norwich*. It has the imprints *Marcus Armstrong, del.*[2] and *I. Royce sculp.*[3]

Description

A small and rather poorly drawn version of the Bucks' North-East Prospect of the city [31], without any references. The dominant features are the spire of the cathedral, and a number of church towers along the horizon. Except in the area of the Cathedral Close, it is no longer possible to trace the pattern of the streets or the walls. The extensive foreground lacks the figures of the Bucks' Prospect, and the general impression is of the city at a distance. The border is formed by two thin lines; above the border is the title, and below the border the dedication *Inscribed to the Mayor and Corporation*. The imprint of Marcus Armstrong is outside the border, bottom left, and the imprint of the engraver outside the border, bottom right.

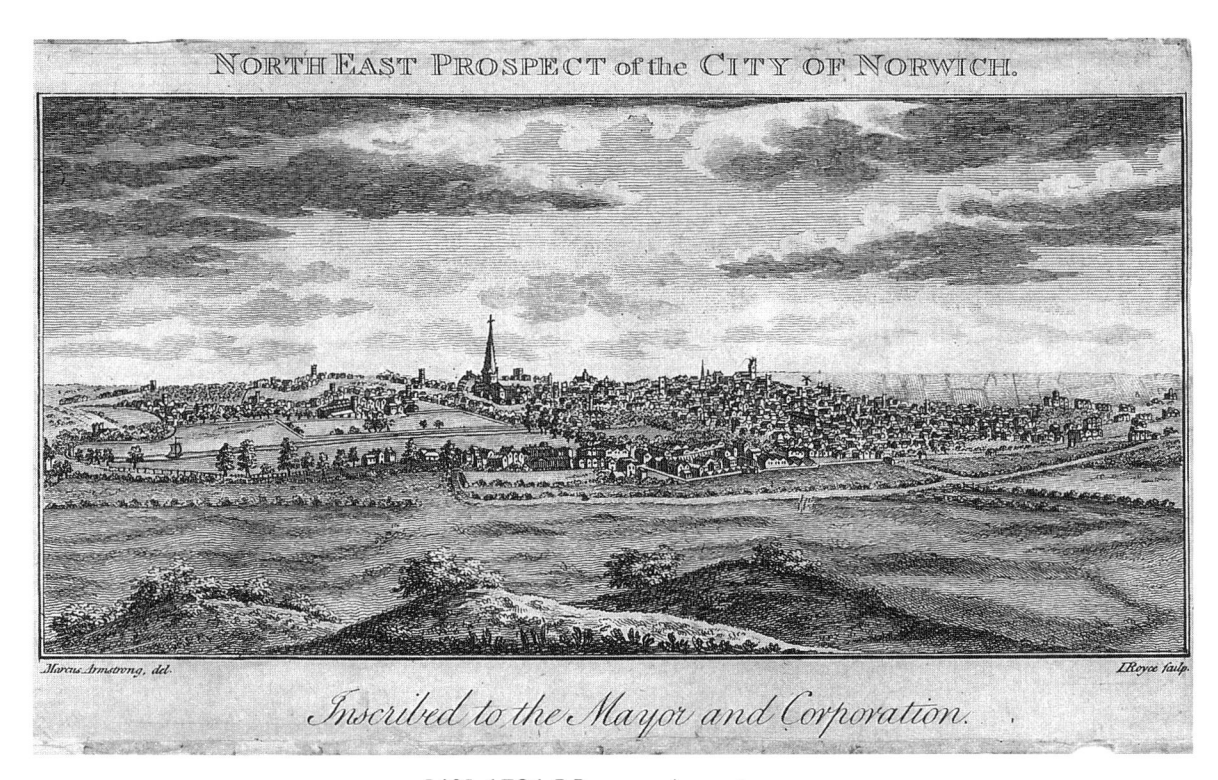

[42] 1781 Marcus Armstrong

1. Not included in Stephen. Examples as for [41].
2. Marcus Armstrong, another member of the Armstrong family, drew a number of the illustrations in the *History*. He apparently then left Norwich, as he produced a four sheet map of Scotland in 1782.
3. John Royce was a London engraver, with an address in Wood Street. A number of different engravers were used for the illustrations in the work.

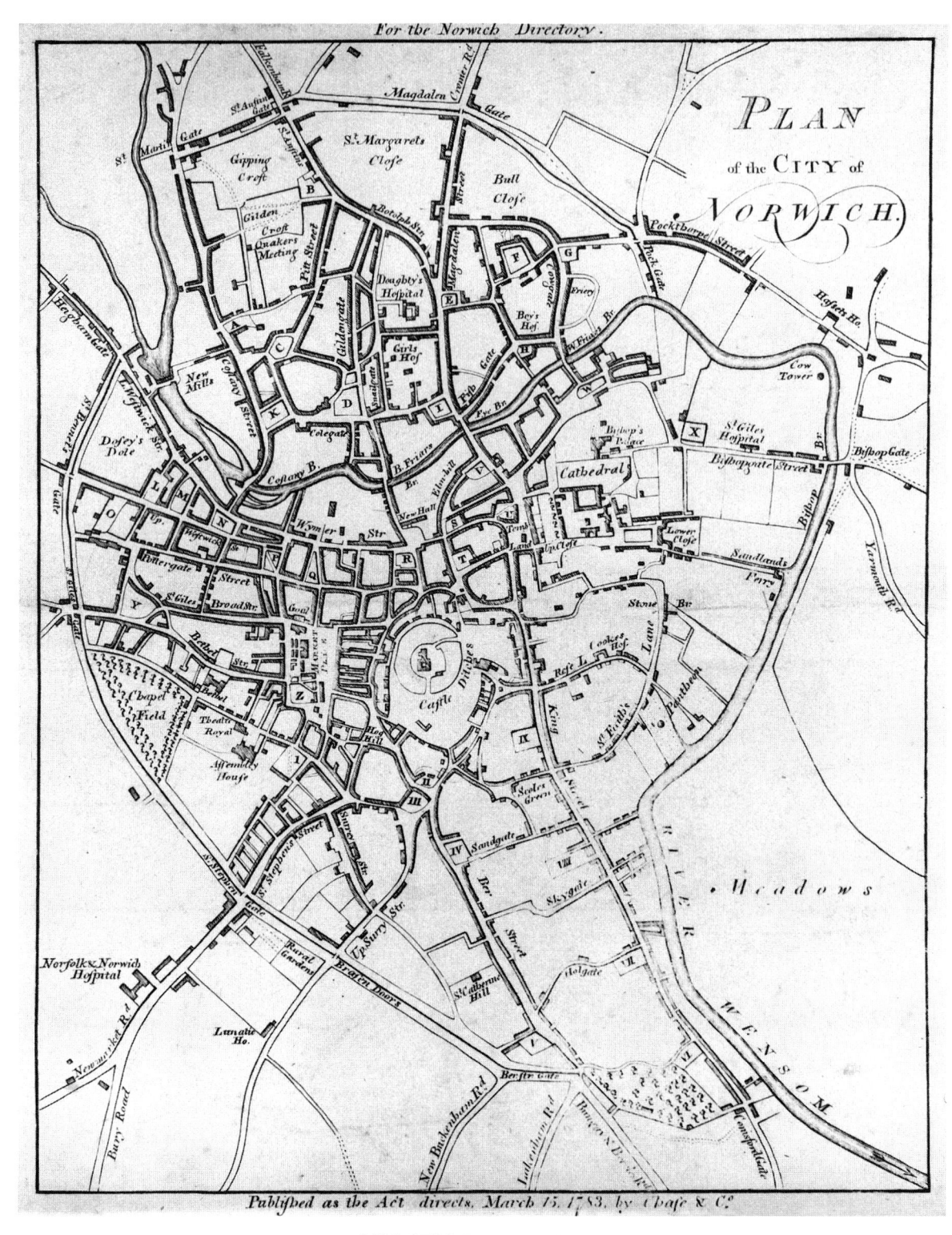

[43] 1783 Thomas Smith

[43] THOMAS SMITH — Norwich — 1783

PLAN of the CITY of NORWICH[1] 225 x 180 mm.

No Scale is shown

Source
From *THE NORWICH DIRECTORY or Gentleman and Tradesmen s Assistant.....With an engraved PLAN of the City; and References..... NORWICH*: Printed and Sold by W. CHASE and Co. March 22, 1783.[2] The plan has outside the top border *For the Norwich Directory.*, and below the bottom border *Published as the Act directs, March 15, 1783, by Chase & C°. Engraved by T. Smith White Lion Lane.*[3]

Description
A neatly engraved plan, with a single line border, and beginning to take on a rather more modern appearance. The city walls are shown as a single line, and the gates named but not illustrated. Churches are indicated by numbers and letters, with the references set out on page (ii) of the *Directory*; the page also lists the gates, and the public buildings, of which most but not all are named on the plan. Street frontages and individual buildings are shown in block form, with the first indications of some very limited development outside the walls This includes for the first time the Norfolk and Norwich Hospital (so named), which had been opened in 1771.

Later History
A further edition of the *Directory* with the same plan was issued in **1784**. The next Directory was that published by Thomas Peck in 1802, with a new plan **[46]**.

1. Stephen p. 215 (1783). BL C.104.dd.20 ; Bod G.A. Norf 80 220 (1); Nfk.Lib.; RCF.
2. For the firm of William Chase &Co. see Norwich Mercury **[25]**, note 2. This is the earliest Norwich Directory to include the names and addresses of the business residents.
3. In the *Directory* Thomas Smith is shown as a Copper Plate and Seal Engraver, at no. 20, White Lion Lane. Because his imprint is at the bottom of the plan below the date of publication, this line is sometimes missing. Smith also engraved the plan in Peck's *Directory* of 1802.

[44] ANTHONY HOCHSTETTER — Norwich — 1789

PLAN of the CITY of NORWICH[1] 590 x 770 mm.

A Scale of Twenty Chains or Eighty Rods = 4.875" (125 mm.) 1:3249 19.5" = 1 mile

Source
A separate publication, with the title *PLAN of the CITY of NORWICH, Describing the Streets, Lanes, Public Edifices & Buildings &c. Divided Into its respective WARDS. Survey'd by Anthony Hochstetter*[2] *and Engrav'd by Samuel John Neele, N°. 352, Strand, LONDON. 1789.*

Origin of the Plan
Hochstetter's intention to produce a new survey of Norwich was announced in the *Norwich Mercury* of 6 January 1787. The scale was to be 20 inches to a mile, the price to subscribers 5s. He invited subscriptions in Norwich to R. Beatniffe, Bookseller, and at the White Swan, King's

[44] 1789 Anthony Hochstetter

Head and Johnson's Coffee House in St.Peter's, and also in Great Yarmouth where he himself was stationed, either to himself or to the booksellers Downes and Marsh. In the *Norwich Mercury* of 27 January 1787 he thanked people for the support which he had received, and said that he would begin the survey as soon as the season would permit.

Description
A very fine plan, engraved by a leading London engraver, the most detailed plan of the city after that of Samuel King **[36]** in 1766, and before that of Millard and Manning **[53]** in 1830. There has been some further development in Pockthorpe, and outside St. Stephen's Gate opposite the Hospital, but otherwise there is still very little new building outside the walls. The border is formed of one outer thick and one thinner line. Top right within the border is the title; top left are the city arms and the dedication, to the mayor, recorder, sheriffs and commonalty of the city ; bottom left are thirty six references to churches, and twenty three references to public buildings; bottom centre is the scale, and bottom right a compass indicator. The alignment of the plan has west-south-west to the top. Beneath the bottom border is the imprint *Published April 23rd. 1789 by Anthony Hochstetter & Sold by B. Beatniffe, Messrs. Berry, Crosers and Stevenson, Norwich, Downes & Marsh, Yarmouth & by the Engraver, London.---- Price 7s.6d.*[3]

Later History
It does not appear that the plan was directly reprinted, and Hochstetter himself seems to have had no further contact with the city. However a lithographic reproduction of the plan was produced towards the end of the 19th century by Jarrold and Sons, from 3, Paternoster buildings London E.C., Norwich, Yarmouth and Cromer, at a price of one shilling.

1. Stephen p. 215, with illustration. BL Maps K.Top.31.33; PRO W 78/7581; CUL Maps bb.77.97.4; Nfk.Lib.; Castle; RCF.
2. Anthony Hochstetter was an Ordnance officer. However he was apparently able to undertake personal commissions, as in the *Norwich Mercury* of 27 November 1784 he advertises himself as *Land Surveyor, surveys and draws plan of Estates...*He was then living in Great Yarmouth, and he says that a specimen of his work could be inspected at Downes and Marsh's, stationers, in that town; it appears that he remained posted to Yarmouth until he left the county. In the *Mercury* of 22 December 1788 he announced, from an address given as the Royal Powder Mills, Feversham, that 'on account of a recent promotion, he is obliged to leave Norfolk'. He said that the plan had been left in the hands of an eminent engraver and was nearly finished. The publication was announced in the *Mercury* on 2nd May 1789; in the *Norfolk Chronicle* of 30th May copies of the plan for 5s. each were offered to anyone who had not originally subscribed, it also being stated that 'Mr. Hochstetter's situation as an officer under the Ordnance, not permitting him to remain longer in Norfolk'.
3. A note on the copy at the PRO indicates that the plan was sold in London by William Faden.

[45] THE POLITICAL MAGAZINE   London   1791

The South East View of Norwich[1]   102 x 181 mm.

Source
From *THE POLITICAL MAGAZINE AND PARLIAMENTARY, NAVAL, MILITARY, AND LITERARY JOURNAL For the Year M,DCC,XCI VOLUME XXI, LONDON. Printed for R. BUTTERS, No.79, FLEET-STREET; and sold by every Bookseller and News-Carrier in GREAT BRITAIN*. The Magazine was published monthly, and the view of Norwich appeared with the issue for October 1791.[2] There is a reference on the first page to the illustrations, but no other references to the views or any accompanying text.

Description

This is a further small prospect or view based on the Bucks' South-East Prospect of the city, and it is a very similar to the Views of Ryland [35] and of Goadby [40]. Minor differences, including the engraving of the sky and clouds, and of the boats on the river, are only apparent on close inspection, and it appears likely that this version of the Prospect was copied from the print produced by Ryland in 1764.

1. Not in Stephen. BL P.P. 3557.v.; Bod Hope adds. 151-169.
2. The Political Magazine was first published in 1742, and continued until 1791; volume XXI containing the View of Norwich was the last. Between 1742 and 1790 the *Magazine* issued 45 maps, including 42 maps of English, Scottish and Irish Counties; that of Norfolk appeared in June 1789,(Chubb p.74). At the front of each of the issues in 1791 were two views of towns and cities; that for October contained a view of Chichester, in addition to that of Norwich. Most of the maps were engraved by John Lodge, but it is not known whether he may also have been responsible for engraving the Views.

[46] JOHN NINHAM　　　　　　　　　　　　　**Norwich**　　　　　　　　　　　　**1802**

PLAN of the CITY of NORWICH[1]　　　　　　　　　　　　　　　　　350 x 285 mm.

No Scale is shown

Source

From *THE Norwich Directory CONTAINING.....A CONCISE HISTORY of NORWICH WITH AN ENGRAVED PLAN of the CITY, with REFERENCES. BY THOMAS PECK.*[2] The Directory is printed and sold by J. Payne Bookseller, 22, Market Place, Norwich.[3] It is dated 1802, but on some copes the date is missing. The plan was *Drawn by J. Ninham*[4] and *Engrav'd by T. Smith Norwich.*[5]

Description

A clearly engraved plan, covering the same area, and with very similar detail to that contained in the plan in the earlier *Directory*, that of 1783 [43], which had also been engraved by Thomas Smith. While John Ninham appears to have copied from the earlier plan, it does have its own style, and a few changes have been made. Most noticeable of these are the addition of the Horse Barracks in Pockthorpe, which dated from 1791, and the Iron Foundry fronting the river first shown on Hochstetter's plan of 1789 [44]. The plan has a double border, each of thin double lines. The title is within the border at the top; the imprints of Ninham and of Smith are within the lower border, to left and right respectively, and in the centre of the lower border *Published as Act directs Feby. 10. 1802 by T. Peck.*

1. Stephen p. 216 (1802). BL C.104.dd.20 ; BL Add. MS 23037.*f*.37; Bod G.A. Norf 80 68 (8); Nfk.Lib.; RCF.
2. The name of Thomas Peck does not itself appear in the *Directory,* which is very similar in layout and content to the *Directory* published by Chase & Co. in 1783, [43].
3. John Payne was a printer in Yarmouth in 1780. He is recorded as being in partnership with Richard Beatniffe in 1798; in the *Directory* Beatniffe is described as a Bookseller, Binder and Stationer in Norwich at 6, Cockey Lane. Payne opened his own shop in 1799 at 53 Market Place, before moving to 22, where in the *Directory* he is also described as Printer, Bookseller and Stationer.
4. John Ninham, (d. 1817), painter and engraver, and father of the Norwich School artist Henry Ninham.
5. Thomas Smith is described in the 1802 *Directory* as an engraver, at 11, Bethel Street.

[47] FRANCIS BLOMEFIELD (2) London 1806

PLAN of the CITY of NORWICH[1] 590 x 475 mm.

No Scale is shown

Source
The plan was published at the front of Volume III of *AN ESSAY TOWARDS A TOPOGRAPHICAL HISTORY OF THE COUNTY OF NORFOLK* by Francis Blomefield, published in London by William Miller in 1806.[2] This is a reprint in eleven volumes of the earlier five volume edition, Volume III having the sub-title *THE HISTORY OF THE CITY AND COUNTY OF NORWICH - PART I*. Norwich comprises Volumes III and IV of the 1806 edition, and the two Norwich volumes were also published separately. Outside the border of the plan, bottom right, is the imprint of the engraver *W Poole direx*[t].[3] Above the border of the plan, top right, is the instruction 'To face Page 1. Vol. 3rd.', and opposite 'To face the Plan' is a page of Explanation, with references to both the numbers on the plan, and to the pages in the volume. The references are the same as those with the 1746 plan, but the page numbers, which are in fact to Volume IV (Norwich Part II), are new to the 1806 edition.

Description
The plan, with single line border, has been directly copied from Blomefield's plan of 1746 [33], without any apparent attempt to update it for any subsequent changes, and with only a very small number of omissions.[4] The plan itself has been reduced in size, to rather less than three quarters of the size of the original. The layout is different, but with the exception of the omission of the dedication, and the scrolls surrounding the title, the description of the city and the coat of arms of the deanery, all the other decorative features have been reproduced in full. The title is top centre, with the city arms and description of the city top left, and the city regalia top right. The other coats of arms, seals, etc., have been rearranged in a different order around the plan. While the copying has been extremely close, there is some difference in the style of the engraving, (particularly noticeable in a comparison of the treatment of the coins), the general effect being that the 1806 plan has an overall lighter appearance than the plan of 1746.

1. Stephen p. 217 (1806). BL 192.c.5-12; Nfk.Lib.; RCF.
2. An announcement was published on 12 October 1804 by W. Miller that a New and Complete Edition of Blomefield's *History* was to be published in ten volumes (plus indexes); the first volume would be ready on the 1st June 1805, the second on the 1st June 1806, then one every four months; subscriptions were to be taken by booksellers in Norwich, Yarmouth, Lynn, and elsewhere in Norfolk, and in Ipswich, Cambridge and Colchester. (BL L.23.c.11.(43.)) . With the exception of the date, and the name of the publisher and printer, the title page has the same detail as in the earlier edition.
3. W. Poole, engraver; other cartographic work included a plan of Reading (of a similar size to the 1806 plan of Norwich) dated 1798, inserted in Charles Coates, *History and Antiquities of Reading*, London, 1802.
4. Close examination shows that a few names, particularly on either side of the city wall, are missing, e.g. Lollards Pit, S[t] Cath[s] Close and the nearby Dove House. As noted by Stephen, the swan mark of Carrow Abbey (number 195 on the Explanation), has been omitted.

[48] GEORGE COLE London 1807

NORWICH[1] 235 x 178 mm.

A Scale of 20 chains (440 yards) = 1.5" (38 mm.)   1:10560   6" = 1 mile

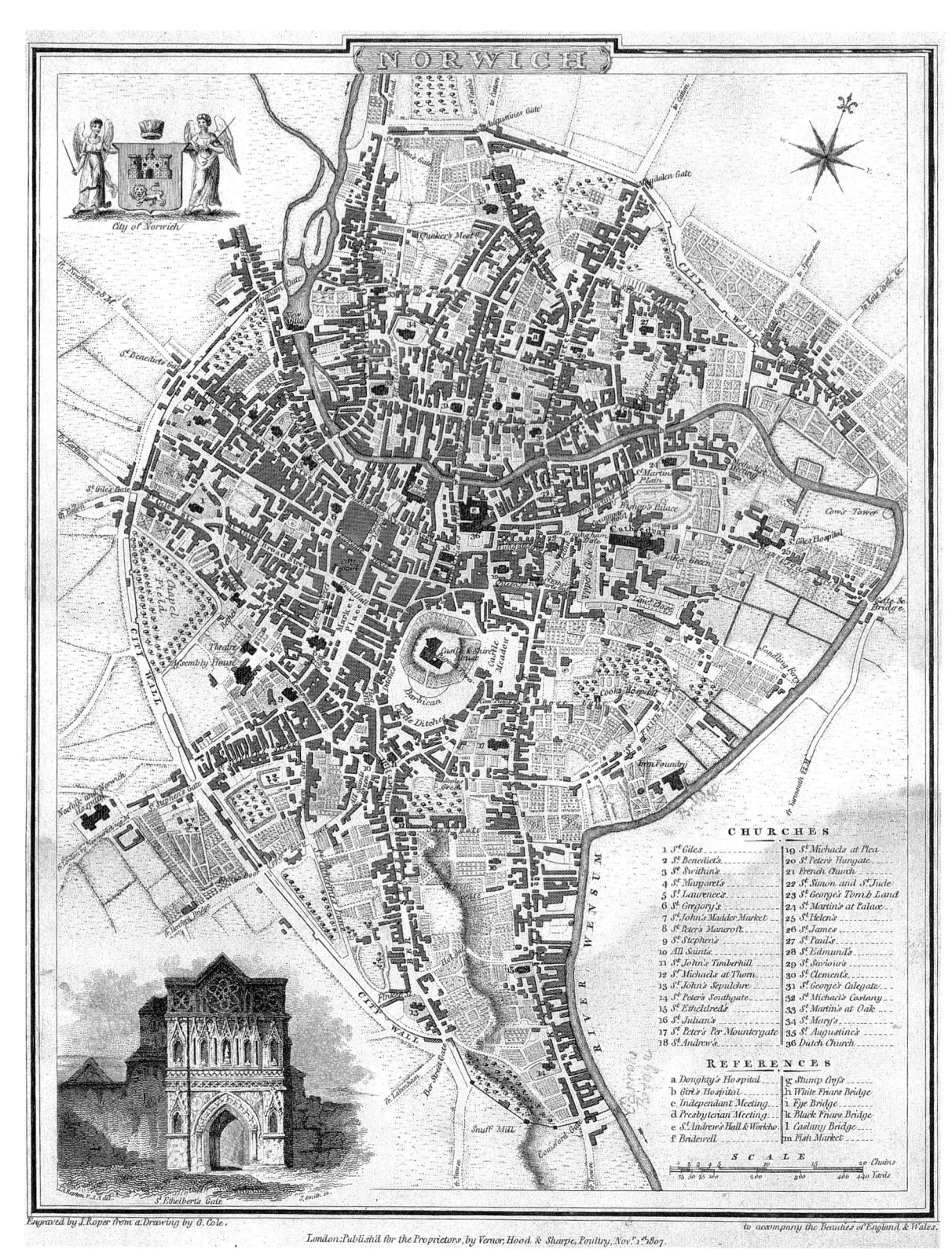

[48] 1807 George Cole

Source

From *The British Atlas; Comprising a complete Series of County Maps; and Plans Of Cities and Principal Towns; Intended to Illustrate And Accompany The Beauties of England and Wales...London: Printed for the Proprietors, And Sold By Vernor, Hood and Sharpe, 31, Poultry; Longman & Co. Paternoster-Row; J. & A. Arch, No 61, Cornhill..*[2]. The *Atlas* was issued in parts, the first on 1 October 1804. The Norwich plan is from Part XVI, dated December 1, 1807, *Price 2s.6d Containing Maps of Lincolnshire and Nottinghamshire, with a Plan of Norwich.* The complete series was brought together in an edition of *The British Atlas; comprising....Plans of Cities and Principal Towns....London.....1810.*

Description

A clearly engraved plan of the city, within a double border, the outer consisting of one thick line between two thin lines, and the inner border of one thin line. The title is within the top border. The plan, which was engraved by J. Roper from a drawing by George Cole,[3] shows considerable detail, not only of the streets and buildings, but strikingly of the gardens and other open areas. There is no suggestion here that this is an original survey, and although it is on a much smaller scale there are very close similarities between the detail shown by Cole and that on the plan of Hochstetter [45]. Each has references to 36 churches, and with the exception that Cole includes the Dutch Church instead of the cathedral included by Hochstetter, they are listed in the same order. Cole has a further 12 references to other features which are also listed by Hochstetter or shown on his plan. In addition to the compass indicator, top right, there are two decorative features, the coat of arms of the city top left, and a drawing of St. Ethelbert's gateway to the Close bottom left. This drawing has separate imprints, *J.A. Repton F.S.A. del.* and *J.Smith sc.* Below and outside the bottom border are the imprints *Engraved by J. Roper from a Drawing by G.Cole,* and *London; Publish'd for the Proprietors by Vernor, Hood and Sharpe, Poultry, Nov*[r]*. 1*[st]*. 1807.* Below the border bottom right are the words *to accompany the Beauties of England and Wales.*

Later History

The plan, without alteration, appears as the frontispiece to *A TOPOGRAPHICAL AND HISTORICAL ACCOUNT OF THE City and County OF NORWICH - NORWICH — PRINTED BY AND FOR JOHN STACY, MARKET-PLACE, AND SOLD BY ALL OTHER BOOKSELLERS IN NORWICH AND NORFOLK AND IN London — BY LONGMAN, HURST, REES, ORME, AND BROWN.* **1819**. A further edition of the *TOPOGRAPHICAL AND HISTORICAL ACCOUNT* was published in **1832**; the plan is unaltered, with the original imprint and date.[4]

1. Stephen p. 217 (1807), p. 218 (1819), p .221(1832).BL Maps 11.b.3 ; Bod C17 c.5 ; Nfk.Lib.; Castle; RCF.
2. Although the maps and the plan state that they were produced to accompany *The Beauties of England and Wales,* the text and the maps were not issued together. Twenty five volumes of the text were completed between 1801 and 1816; the maps and plans were published in parts from October 1804, the last part dated October 1, 1808. The map of Norfolk, also engraved by J. Roper from a drawing by Cole, is dated March 1, 1808, (Chubb p. 86). For the text relating to Norfolk, published in Volume XI, see the Later History of *The South-East View of the City of Norwich,* Goadby [40].
3. George Cole, active 1796 - 1830 in drawing estate and other maps; see Bendall, *Dictionary of Land Surveyors.*
4. In the 1832 edition the address of John Stacy is now Old Haymarket, and the London names are Longman, Rees, Orme, Brown and Green.

[49]   HAROLD ASTON BARKER   Norwich   **1809**

Panoramic View of the CITY of NORWICH AND SURROUNDING COUNTRY with a Perspective View of the Castle and County Gaol[1]   465 x 335 mm.

Source
A separate publication, a coloured engraving on a single sheet, containing in the upper part a panoramic view of the city, and in the lower part a perspective view of the castle. The views are *TO HIS MAJESTY'S JUSTICES of the PEACE, For the County of Norfolk....respectfully inscribed by their obedient Servants W. Stevenson, J. Matchett, and S. W. Stevenson,* and *Norwich, Published as the Act Directs, by Stevenson, Matchett and Stevenson, Sep.1.1809.*

Description
An original panoramic view of the city as seen from the castle. Forming a border along the sides and the top of the plate are references by numbers to ' the principal objects seen from the hill'. Particularly clearly seen are the cathedral, St. Peter Mancroft and a number of other churches, the entrance gateway to the castle, and various properties around the base of the hill. The fine perspective view of the castle is taken from the south east; beneath the view are the names of the artist, *H.A.Barker del*[2], and of the engraver, *Williams Sculp*.

1. Stephen p. 218 (1809), with illustration. BL Maps K.Top.31.34.i.; BL Add. MS 23037.f.62 (proof); Nfk.Lib.(proof); Castle.
2. Harold Aston Barker, 1774-1861, son of Robert Barker, 1739-1806, an Irish born artist, who invented the technique of 360 degree painting which he patented in 1787, and coined the name Panorama in 1791. Between 1793 and 1863 the Barker family ran the Rotunda in Leicester Square for the exhibition of Panoramas. H.A.Barker worked almost exclusively as an artist on panoramas from the age of 12, and ran the family business from his father's death until his retirement in 1822. See R.Hyde, *Panoramania,* London, 1988.

[50]   THOMAS STARLING   London   **1819**

NORWICH[1]   190 x 145 mm.

A Scale of 20 chains (440 yards) = 1.187" (30 mm.)   1:13339   4.75" = 1 mile

Source
Inserted as the front page in Volume II of *EXCURSIONS IN THE COUNTY OF NORFOLK* printed in London for Longman, Hurst, Rees, Orme and Brown: J.Greig, Upper Street Islington; and P.Youngman, Witham and Maldon, Essex, and dated 1819. The plan has the imprints *Engraved by T. Starling Islington London,* and *Published May 1st. 1819 by Messrs. Longman & Co. Paternoster Row.*

Description (State 1)
The plan is so similar to the plan of Cole **[48]**, that it is clearly based on it. The plan is smaller, but the details, and the wording, are almost identical.[2] Similarly the outer border has a thick line between two thin lines, and an inner border one thin line. The title is within the top border, the compass indicator is above the actual plan top right, and the 36 references to churches and the 12 references to other features are the same as in the earlier plan, the former bottom right, and the latter bottom left, above the scale. Outside the bottom border are the publisher's imprint, and, to the right, the name of the engraver.

Later History
The plan was revised for inclusion in *The Beauties of England and Wales...Vol. XXX. Norfolk. London: Printed for J. Harris; Longman & Co..&c.* The work itself is not dated, but the imprint on the plan gives the date as **1826**.

Description (State 2)
A number of alterations have been made.[2] The 'References' have been increased in number from 12 to 21. The scale has been moved to within the bottom border, and the imprint is now *Published Jany. 1. 1826*

1. Stephen p. 219 (1819), and p.220 (1826). BL 564.d.10 ; BL Add. MS 23037.f.38 ; Bod Gough Gen Top 259; Nfk.Lib.; RCF.
2. Close comparison reveals some omissions, e.g. the naming of Bigod's Tower at the Castle, and the Bethel, and the reference to the snuff mill outside the city wall. There has been some attempt to update the plan, and additions include the Duke's Palace bridge, the new bridge by the Iron Foundry, the Crescent, and the site for the new city gaol.

[51]   RICHARD TAYLOR (1)   London   1821

Map of NORWICH previous to the dissolution of the MONASTERIES[1]   430 x 275 mm.

A Scale of 20 Chains = 2.125" (53 mm.)   1:7454   8.5" = 1 mile

Source
From *Index Monasticus; or THE ABBEYS AND OTHER MONASTERIES.....FORMERLY ESTABLISHED IN The Diocese of Norwich....AND ILLUSTRATED BY MAPS OF Suffolk, Norfolk and the City of Norwich — by RICHARD TAYLOR OF NORWICH.*[2] *LONDON: PRINTED FOR THE AUTHOR, BY RICHARD AND ARTHUR TAYLOR, SHOE LANE; SOLD BY MESSRS. LACKINGTON AND COMPANY, FINSBURY SQUARE, J. AND A. ARCH, CORNHILL, AND RODWELL AND MARTIN, NEW BOND STREET; AND BY MESSSRS. STEVENSON, MATCHETT AND STEVENSON, NORWICH. — 1821.*[3]

Description
A clearly engraved plan of the city, with the gates and line of the city walls, the pattern of the roads within the walls, and the roads leaving the city with their former destinations (e.g. to Bromholm Priory), the castle, the cathedral, churches and the sites of the mediaeval monastic establishments. Taylor says in his introduction that care has been taken where practicable to describe the exact situation or position of the monasteries, but in many instances, especially in the early religious houses the precise sites are unknown The plan extends beyond the walls to the north to show the leper houses, to the east to include the site of St. Leonard's Priory, and to the south Carrow Priory. A summary, top right, refers to 138 establishments inside and a further 15 establishments outside the walls, excluding many small chapels. To the bottom left of the plan is the title, with the scale below; to the right is a compass rose. The wide border is made up of one thick and a number of thin lines, with hatching between the inner and outer lines. Within the bottom border are the imprints *Drawn by Rich^d. Taylor* and *Engraved by Neele & Son, 352, Strand.*[4]

1. Stephen p. 220 (1821). BL 1896.c.44; BL Add. MS 23037.f.31; Bod K 5.353; Nfk.Lib.; RCF. Taylor's manuscript draft of the plan is in the Todd collection in the Castle.

2. Richard Cowling Taylor, 1789 - 1851, was born at Banham, Norfolk on 18 January 1789. Taylor was primarily a geologist and mining engineer, and as such was a member of the principal scientific societies both in England and America. He was associated with William Smith, 'the father of British geology'; he worked for the Ordnance Survey, was employed on surveying for the British Iron Company and other mining companies, and from the 1830s until his death had a distinguished scientific career in America. While in Norfolk he wrote a number of articles on local geology, and was concerned with the proposals for the improvement of navigation between Norwich and Lowestoft (leading to the creation of the New Cut at Haddiscoe). Taylor developed an early interest in the monastic remains in Norfolk and Suffolk, and his scholarship and scientific background is evident in his writing; the success of the *Index Monasticus* led to a request to undertake the production of a General Index to Dugdale's *Monasticon Anglicanum*, which was published in 1830, shortly before his departure for America.
3. Richard Taylor issued proposals for publishing the *INDEX MONASTICUS* in August 1819 , '£1.11.6d. small paper, and £2.12.6d. large paper, the maps engraved by Mr. Neele, from booksellers in London, Norwich, Ipswich and Cambridge.' (BL L .23.c.11.(45.)).
4. The Neele family carried on business as a leading firm of engravers at 352, Strand, during the latter part of the 18th and first half of the 19th centuries.

[52] RICHARD TAYLOR (2)   London   1821

NORDOVICUM: ANGLIAE. CIVITAS[1]   290 x 405 mm.

Source

The plan was produced as a separate item by Richard Taylor, and is sometimes found as an additional map or plan in his *Index Monasticus,* see **[51]**. As well as having been drawn by Taylor, it also has his imprint *Etch^d. by R. Taylor.*

Description

Beneath the title is the explanatory description that the plan is *Compiled from the Perspective maps in Cunynghams Cosmographical Glasse, A.D.1559, and Braun's Urbium Principuarum Totius Mundi A.D.1577 - by Richard Taylor.* Taylor must have had before him in drafting this plan the earlier plans of both Cuningham **[1]** and of Braun and Hogenberg **[2]**. The basis of Taylor's plan is that of Cuningham, but with added features from Braun and Hogenberg , in particular the two figures in Elizabethan dress in the foreground. Some features have been named on the plan , but additionally below the border are 49 references to churches, gates, etc., identified on the plan by numbers.[3]

1. Stephen p. 219 (1821). BL Add. MS 23037,*f*.34; Nfk.Lib.; Castle.
2. The plan seems to have been an afterthought. It was not referred to in the prospectus for the *Index Monasticus*, and is not mentioned in the title or the text. The maps and plan in the *Index* were engraved by Neele, whereas this plan is an etching by Taylor himself. The drawing of the plan is however consistent with Taylor's interest in the city's past, and the importance which he expressed in his writing for maps and plans generally.
3. A copy of the plan in the Todd collection in the Castle lacks the explanatory description and the numbered references, and appears to have been a proof.

[53] WILLIAM SALTER MILLARD AND JOSEPH MANNING   Norwich   1830

Plan of the City of Norwich[1]   1275 x 1015 mm.

A Scale of 12 Chains = 4.937" (125 mm.)   1:1924   32.93" = 1 mile

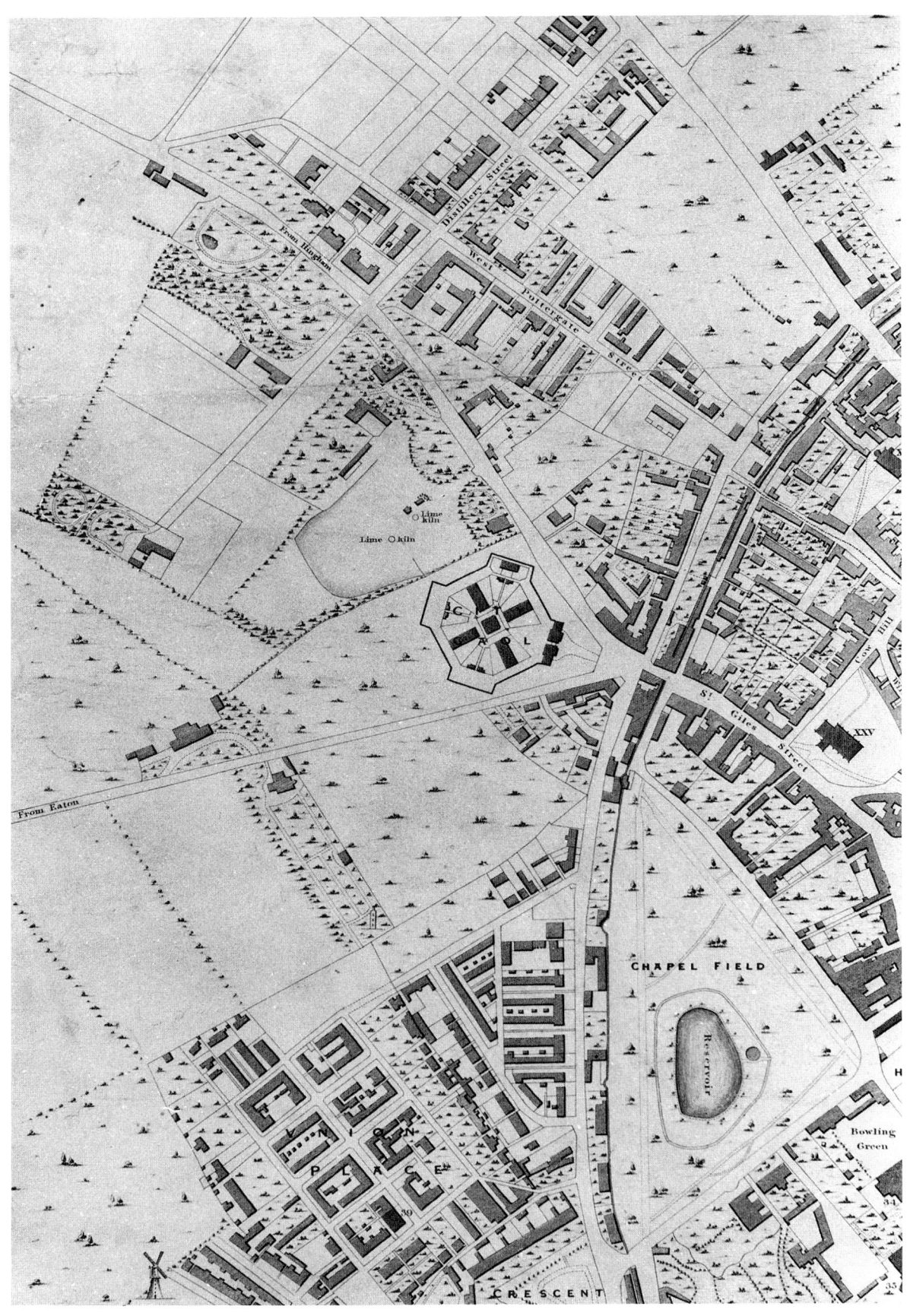

[53] 1830 William Millard and Joseph Manning
(Detail from north western section showing development outside the wall)

Source
A separate publication, a plan of the city *Surveyed by W. S. Millard*[2] *and Jos*[h]*. Manning,*[3] *engraved by J. Dallinger*[4] *, 1830.*

Origin of the Plan
W. S. Millard was commissioned by the General Assembly of the Corporation to carry out a new large scale survey of the city, in which he was assisted by Joseph Manning. John Stacy, printer, Norwich, published Proposals for the survey to be engraved, and published by subscription as *A New and Accurate Survey*. The price to subscribers was one guinea, and subscriptions were to be received by the principal booksellers in the city. For further particulars and a view of the plan, application was to be made to Mr. Millard, Princes' Street, and Mr. Manning, Julian Place, near Chapel Field.[5]

Description
The first detailed survey of the city after that by Hochstetter [44] in 1789, and the most important plan of the city in the first half of the 19th century. The scale is such that individual buildings are shown, and comparison can readily be made with Hochstetter's plan to identify developments which had taken place during the previous 40 years.[6] Unlike the later plan of Manning alone [55] this plan does not extend to the outer boundaries of the county of the city; it is of the city within the line of the walls, but also shows that the city was beginning to extend beyond the walls. This is particularly noticeable to the west, with the new residential areas, some such as the Crescent which has survived, but much of which became areas of bomb damage and of slum clearance in the 20th century. That said, the overall impression is still of comparatively little building outside the traditional city centre, and of open country in those areas out towards the outer boundaries of the county of the city which were to be developed during the next hundred years.

The plan was engraved in four sheets. It has an outer border of one thick between two thin lines, and an inner border of two thin lines. Top left is the title. Top right are the city arms, with the dedication, *To the Right Worshipful The Mayor The Alderman Sheriffs and Commonalty of the city of Norwich This Survey made by their direction is respectfully dedicated By their obliging and Obedient Servant W.S.Millard*. A table of references, right, includes churches from I to XXXV, and public buildings from 1 to 42. Bottom left is the scale, references to the wards, and a compass indicator, NNW to the top.

1. Stephen p. 221 (1830). Nfk.Lib.; Castle.
2. William Salter Millard, leading Norwich land surveyor; was appointed Steward of the estates of the Bethel Hospital (*Chronicle* 7 Nov 1807); appointed by the Corporation to conduct a survey; and a Report on duties, salaries, and emoluments of the late officers of the Corporation - 'Mr W. S. Millard land surveyor has no salary but was paid by his charges for surveys and plans He is also Surveyor of the Hospital and Charity Estates' (*Mercury* 13 February 1836). He was joined by his son Charles William Millard, admitted freeman 24 February 1835, and they continued to practice as Wm. Salter Millard & Son, land agents, in Princes' Street.
3. Joseph Manning, surveyor in practice from various addresses in Norwich; advertised (*Mercury* 5 April 1828) that he had been exclusively employed in practice in Norwich as a land surveyor from 1819; moved to Julian Place in 1828, (*Chronicle* 4 October 1828); in Bethel Street in 1836, advertising for surveying, valuations for commutation of tithes, parish assessments, etc., from Norwich and Eye; in 1837 appointed by the Board of Governors of the Hartismere Union, Suffolk, to survey and map all such parishes as shall be requested by the Board (*Chronicle* 25 November 1837).
4. Joseph Dallinger, in business as an engraver at 18 Davey Place, Norwich (Pigot's *Directory* 1830); also referred to as a lithographer (White's *Directory,* 1836).
5. The Proposals, which are not dated, state 'The numerous and important improvements which have taken place, or are now in progress in the City and PORT of Norwich, will, it is presumed, make this a work of considerable interest.' (Norfolk & Norwich Archaeological Society Library).
6. For example the new gas works, the proposed widening of the river and the new basin for sea going vessels.

[54] ROBERT KEARSLEY DAWSON London 1832

NORWICH From the Ordnance Survey[1] 300 x 350 mm.

A Scale of 2 Inches (50 mm.) to 1 Mile   1:31680

Source
The plan is one of a series of plans specially prepared by Lieutenant Dawson[2] for the purposes of the Boundary Commission, whose Report including the plan was ordered to be published in 1832. It appeared in the *Report from Commissioners on Proposed (Parliamentary) Division of Counties and Boundaries of Boroughs Vol. II, Part II, 20th. January 1832.*[3] The name of the printer is below the plan, *R. Cartwright, Lithog. Warwick Pl. Bedford Row.* The total of 227 lithographic maps and plans were then printed together in two volumes with the title *Plans of the Cities and Boroughs of England and Wales: shewing their boundaries as established by the Boundaries' Act, passed 11th July 1832: together with Outline Maps' shewing' the division of counties, the principal places of election, and the polling places, as established by the same Act. In two volumes, London.: Printed by James & Luke G. Hansard & Sons, near Lincoln's Inn Fields, 1832.* The plan of Norwich is number 121 in Volume I.

Origin of the Plan
In the preparation of the borough plans Dawson was able to make use of the work of the Ordnance Survey, by whom he was employed. The area of Norfolk covering the city of Norwich had not then been published, but Norwich had been surveyed as long ago as in 1817 on a scale of 2 inches to a mile. Dawson's plan is copied from the unpublished Ordnance Survey map, and repeats its mistakes.[3]

Description
This is the first listed plan of the county of the city within its outer boundary. The plan is intended to show the former and proposed new boundary, by green and red coloured lines respectively. In fact in the case of Norwich no changes were proposed, the Commissioners advising that they were of the opinion that the present boundaries were satisfactory.[4] As the plan was directed towards establishing the outer boundary, the area within the line of the walls is less detailed. It is interesting in showing that there was still at the time comparatively little development within the outer hamlets, see Manning [55]. The plan gives the names only of the outer suburbs of Catton, Thorpe, Trowse Newton and Keswick. Beneath the title to the right of the plan is the signature *Robert K. Dawson Lieut. R.E.*[5]

1. Stephen p. 221 (1832). BL Maps 149.d.28; BL 23037.*f*.39; Bod Maps C.17.a.20-21; Nfk.Lib.
2. Robert Kearsley Dawson, 1798-1861, was the son of Robert Dawson, 1771-1860, who had a long career with the Ordnance Survey. He was commissioned into the Royal Engineers in 1818, and followed his father into the Ordnance Survey, working under Major General Colby in Scottish and Irish surveys. In the early 1830s Dawson was entrusted with the task of preparing a set of county maps, and plans of all the boroughs of England and Wales.
3. BL Maps, original surveyor's drawing 241. Mistakes in the original survey include Easton for Eaton, and Wenson for Wensum; these are copied without correction by Dawson.
4. 'We have reason to believe that the limits of the City and the County thereof are perfectly well known and undisputed. We are of the opinion that the present limits of the City of Norwich are satisfactory, and should be the same as have been heretofore known as the Boundaries and limits of the City and the County of the City of Norwich, including such extra parochial places as are within the Boundary and the Castle.' BL Add. MS 23037.*f*.40.
5. What appears to be a proof copy of the plan is in the Todd collection in the Castle; it is without Dawson's signature, and without the explanation of the colouring.

[55] c.1834 Joseph Manning
(By Permission of the Syndics of Cambridge University Library - Maps c.77.83.1)

[55] JOSEPH MANNING   Norwich   c. 1834

PLAN of the City and County of NORWICH[1]   650 x 735 mm.

A Scale of 40 Chains = 3.437" (87 mm.)   1:9217   6.874" = 1 mile

Source
A separate publication by Joseph Manning,[2] with the imprint *ENGRAVED BY JOSIAH NEELE, 352, STRAND, LONDON.*[3]

Origin of the Plan
Manning had been associated with W. S. Millard in the production of the larger scale map of the city **[53]** in 1830. This present plan is not merely a reduced and revised version of the earlier publication, and it seems likely that Manning will have completed the survey for this plan following the completion of the earlier survey.[4]

Description
This is the first large scale plan to show in detail the whole of the area within the outer boundary of the county of the city. In addition to the outer boundary itself, the plan shows the boundaries of the wards. Although the plan of the city within the walls follows, on a smaller scale, the earlier plan of Millard and Manning, there are important differences in treatment, in part necessitated by the difference in scale. There are parts of the city where detail seems to have been deliberately omitted, e.g. the area between Ber Street and King Street. However full details are shown of the large areas of land, mostly still undeveloped, outside the line of the walls. It makes it very clear that the hamlets of Eaton, Earlham, and Lakenham in particular, are still very small communities well away from the main centre of the city's population. However an added interest is in the names of the owners of the principal residences, and of the mainly agricultural estates which were the scene of rapid development in the coming years. The two plans, this and the earlier plan can therefore be seen as complementary, and together provide much the most complete picture of the city as a whole at a key point of time in the city's development.
Outside the city plan, but within the borders of a thick and thinner line, are top left, the title, top right, a view of the Castle from Thorpe Road, centre right, 83 References in two columns, churches and public buildings, bottom right, the city arms, and bottom left, the compass points and scale.

1. Stephen p. 222 (1834 ?). CUL Maps c.77.83.1; PRO T 72/3; Nfk.Lib.
2. For Joseph Manning see Millard and Manning **[53]**, note 3.
3. Josiah Neele, publisher and engraver; one of the several members of the Neele family, in the business of engravers at 352, Strand.
4. For a possible connection between Manning's plan and the plan of Kemp and Nichols see **[57]**, note 4.

[56]   WILLIAM PINNOCK   London   1835

NORWICH[1]   230 x 165 mm.

A Scale of 1/4 of a Mile = 1.5" (38 mm.)   1:10560   6" = 1 mile

Source
From *THE GUIDE TO KNOWLEDGE Edited by W. PINNOCK . VOL. III . LONDON 1835.*

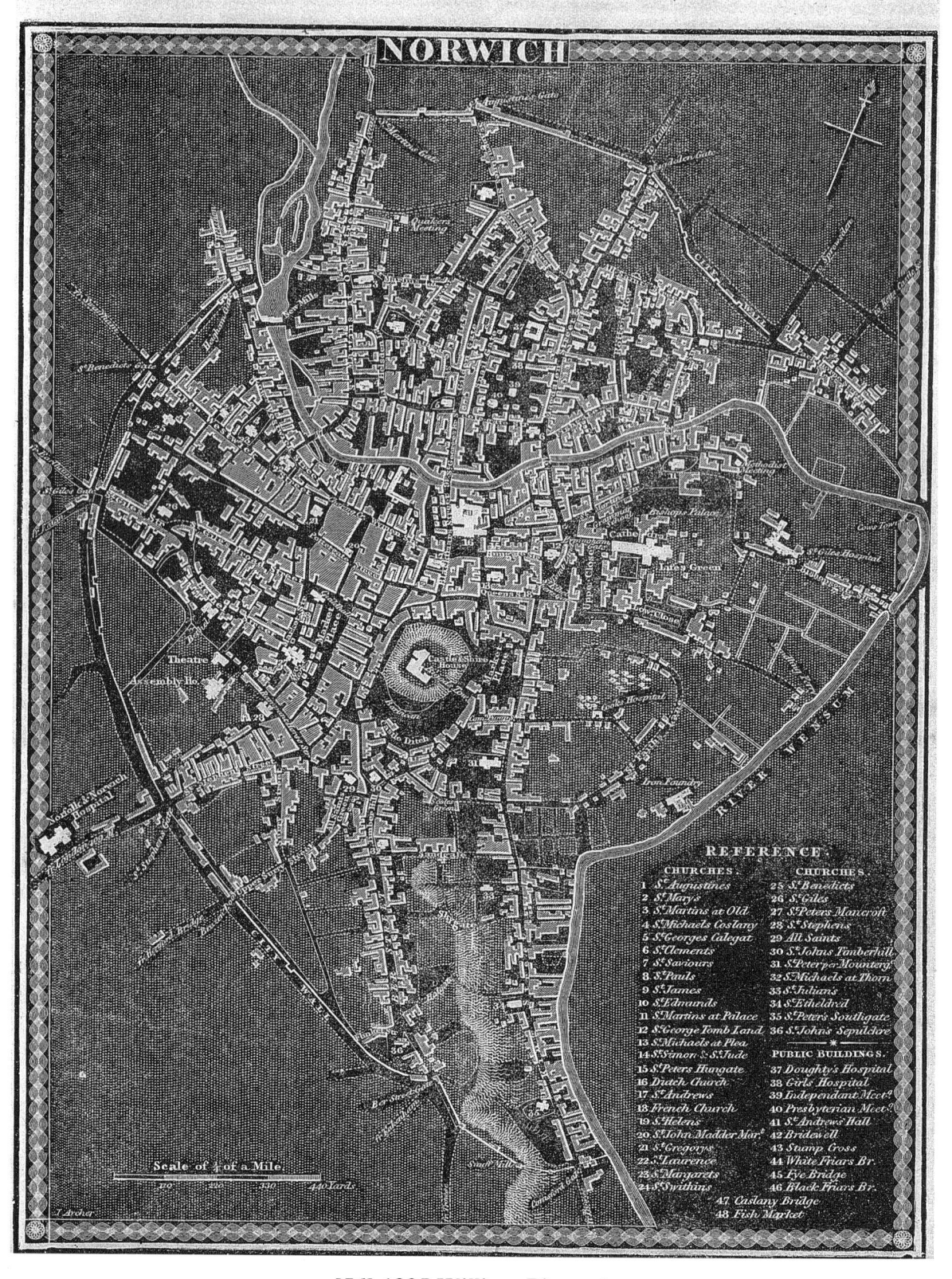

[56] 1835 William Pinnock

Printed for the Proprietors, and Published at their office 2, Wellington Street, Strand; and by W.Edwards, 12, Ave Maria Lane. 1835.[2] The plan, which is in a Supplement to the *Guide*, is signed by the engraver, *J. Archer.*[3]

Description

The plan is unique, in that it is printed in black on white. Thus the writing, and principal buildings such as the cathedral and the castle, appear as white against a dark background. The title is top centre, within a decorative surrounding border; there is a direction indicator top right, 48 references bottom right, and the scale bottom left. The name of the engraver is within the border bottom left. Above the top border are the headings *SUPPLEMENT TO PINNOCK'S GUIDE TO KNOWLEDGE*, and on either side *No.CLXXXV*, and *PRICE ONE PENNY.* Along a margin on the reverse is *R.Clay; Printer, 7, Bread street Hill, Cheapside.*

The plan itself closely resembles that of Cole of 1807 **[48]**, from which it appears to have been copied. It is to the same scale as Cole's plan, and the 48 references are also the same, although in a different order. Both wrongly spell Coslany as Caslany, but Pinnock's plan has other errors, e.g. 'S^t. Martin's at Old' for 'S^t. Martin's at Oak'. The plan has not been updated, and the two new bridges, Foundry and Carrow, are not shown.

1. Not in Stephen. BL P.P.6000.b; BL Add. MS 23057,*f*.6; Nfk.Lib.; RCF.
2. William Pinnock, 1782-1843, was born in Hampshire, and was a schoolmaster before becoming a bookseller in Alton and Newbury. He moved to London in 1817, where he was described as a master printer. Publication of *The Guide to Knowledge* began with weekly parts in 1833, with maps engraved on wood by Joshua Archer and Sidney Hall. Volume I of the *Guide* contains a map of Norfolk, Chubb p. 117 (1833).
3. Joshua Archer, draughtsman and prolific map engraver, of Pentonville, London.

[57] KEMP AND NICHOLS London 1835

MAP OF THE BOROUGH OF NORWICH[1] 380 x 485 mm.

A Scale of 2 miles = 6.687" (170 mm.)   1:18950   3.344" = 1 mile

Source

The title of the map indicates its origin: the map was *as determined by the Commissioners Appointed by the Honourable the Commons House of Parliament 1835* and was *published by Kemp and Nichols Land Surveyors London April 1835.*[2] The only copies of the plan which have been seen are in the PRO, in a file with other plans and documents relating to the work of the Boundary Commission. The plan appears therefore to have been an official publication, and no evidence has been found that it was on sale generally.[3]

Description

A finely engraved uncoloured plan of the whole of the city within its outer boundaries, with references to the wards, with similarities to the plan of Manning **[55]**, on which this plan could have been based.[4] The surrounding edges of the plan consist of a thick line between two thin lines. Top left is the extended title; below left is a compass indicator, references, and the scale. There is also a note that 'The first Members returned to Parliament by this Borough under the Reform Bill were R.Gurney and R. Grant Es^{qrs}.1832.'[5]

1. Not in Stephen. PRO T 72/13.

2. George Kemp, Land Surveyor, whose various published maps include *Ten Miles round Harrogate*, 1832; John Bowyer Nichols, carrying on business as J.B.Nichols and Son, London publisher, whose work included a number of cartographic books and large county histories.

3. There are two copies of the plan at the PRO under reference T 72/13. Under the same reference and in the same file is a small draft plan at a scale of 4" to a mile of the central area of the city, to which is attached a small manuscript draft. There is no evidence of their authorship, or their connection with the Kemp and Nichols plan, but they also clearly relate to the work of the Boundary Commission. It seems likely that Dawson may well have had access to these, and the Kemp and Nichols plan, in drafting his two plans of the city published in 1837, [60] and [61].

4. It may be significant that also in the PRO file is a copy of the plan by Manning.

5. Richard Hanbury Gurney and Robert Grant were in fact elected members for the city in 1830, at the election held consequent on the death of William IV. The first election after the passing of the Reform Act took place in December 1832, those elected being Lord Stormont and Sir James Scarlett.

[58] R CREIGHTON   London   1835

NORWICH[1]   90 x 95 mm.

A Scale of 1½ miles = 1.125" (29 mm.)   1:56320   0.75" = 1 mile

Source
From *A TOPOGRAPHICAL DICTIONARY OF ENGLAND....THIRD EDITION. WITH A SUPPLEMENTARY VOLUME COMPRISING A REPRESENTATIVE HISTORY OF ENGLAND, WITH PLANS DESCRIBING THE ELECTORAL DIVISIONS OF THE SEVERAL COUNTIES, AND THE FORMER AND PRESENT BOUNDARIES OF THE CITIES AND BOROUGHS. BY SAMUEL LEWIS. IN FIVE VOLUMES. Vol.III....M.DCCC.XXXV.* The Supplementary Volume was also published as *VIEW OF THE REPRESENTATIVE HISTORY OF ENGLAND, WITH ENGRAVED PLANS, SHEWING THE ELECTORAL DIVISIONS OF THE SEVERAL COUNTIES...CITIES AND BOROUGHS. BY SAMUEL LEWIS. LONDON: PUBLISHED BY S.LEWIS...1835.* The Norwich plan, together with plans of Thetford, Great Yarmouth and King's Lynn are on page LX, with the imprints *Drawn by R. Creighton*[2] and *Engraved by J. & C. Walker.*[3]

Origin of the Plan
The plan is designed to show changes (if any) in the boundaries of the city as resulting from the recommendations of the Municipal Boundary Commission. It is therefore based on Dawson's plan of 1832, which was in turn based on the original Ordnance Survey of 1817.

Description
The plan, which occupies the top left section of the plate, shows the city within the outer boundary. It is coloured in outline to show the old and new boundaries, although in the case of Norwich no changes were recommended.[4] The errors in the Ordnance Survey plan have been repeated, e.g. Easton for Eaton, and Wenson for Wensum. Outside the city boundary are top left, the title, top right, a compass indicator, and bottom right, the scale. The plate has a decorative border, with three thin lines creating the internal divisions between the plans.

Later History The *Topographical Dictionary* with the plans was reissued dated **1837,** and an edition of the *View Of The Representative History* with plans was published in **1840**.[5] The Fifth Edition of the *Topographical Dictionary*, dated 1842, included county maps, and a plan of London, but not plans of the other cities and boroughs.

1. Stephen p. 223 (1837). BL RB.31.b.106; Nfk.Lib.; RCF.
2. R. Creighton, draughtsman, whose work included county maps for Christopher and John Greenwood's *Atlas of the Counties of England,* London, 1834.
3. J. and C. Walker carried on an important business in London as engravers, draughtsmen and publishers, including work for the East India Company and the Admiralty. They engraved the map of Norfolk for Greenwood's *Atlas.*
4. In some copies the plans have additional overall colour.
5. CUL Atlas 5.84.20.

[59] **WILLIAM IONN**   **Norwich**   **1836**

**ROUTES FROM The City OF Norwich /
THROUGH THE County OF Norfolk**[1]   190 x 245 mm.

Source
A separate publication. Below the plan is the imprint *Published by W*[m]*. Ionn, Norwich 1*[st]*. Dec*[r]*. 1836.*[2]

Description
An interesting and unusual coloured plan, showing the roads from the city in sixteen panels. Each of the panels states the destination of the road, and intermediate distances of villages along the way. The panels surround the plan, which marks the outer boundary of the county of the city. The area inside the boundary is shown as *THE CITY LIBERTY*. This plan is also notable as the first of the listed city plans to show the line of a proposed railway. The line follows the east side of the Ipswich Road, around the south east of the city to Whitlingham, but with no indication of a station within the city itself. The *Explanation,* which occupies the two bottom corners, refers to the railroad, with the note that *It will enter the County a little East of Scole Inn.*[3] The title is divided between the top left and top right corners. The border is formed by a thick and thin line, with an inner line.

1. Stephen p.223 (1836). Nfk.Lib.; Castle.
2. There is no reference to William Ionn as being in business in Norwich in either Pigot's *Commercial Directory* of 1830, or White's *Directory* of 1836, and no other publications by him have been traced.
3. Plans by the Eastern Counties Railway for a line from London to Norwich and Yarmouth were approved in 1836; for various reasons progress was extremely slow, and the line from Ipswich was eventually built in a different position, entering the county at Diss. Meanwhile the Norwich and Yarmouth Railway was established, the line, the first to the city, being opened in 1844.

Illustration   Plate 3

[60] **ROBERT K DAWSON   (Small)**   **London**   **1837**

NORWICH[1]   105 x 110 mm.

A Scale of 1 Inch (25 mm.) to a Mile   1:63360

Source
This plan, and the next plan **[61]**, which are the work of Lieutenant Dawson,[2] are both engraved on the same plate. They were published in a *Report of Commissioners appointed to report and*

advise upon the (Municipal) Boundaries and Wards of Certain Boroughs and Towns England and Wales Part II,. 25th April 1837. The section of the Report which includes the two plans is entitled *REPORT upon the PROPOSED DIVISION into WARDS of the CITY of NORWICH.*

Description

The plan shows the city within its outer boundary, and is similar to Dawson's earlier plan of 1832 **[54]**. However it does not repeat its mistakes, and Dawson may well have had access to the re-survey by the Ordnance Survey in 1836. The purpose of the plans is to show the boundaries of the eight wards as proposed, identified by different colours. This plan shows, outside the inner city, the hamlets of Pockthorpe, Thorpe, Lakenham, Eaton, Earlham, Heigham and Hellesdon. The title, scale and compass direction indicator are to the left of the plans, with the signature below of *R:K:Dawson Lt R.E*. This plan occupies the upper part of the plate, above plan **[61]**.

1. Stephen p. 223 (1837). BL Maps 27.a.27 (Plan); BL Maps 27.d.3 (Report); BL Add. MS 23037.*f*.39; Nfk.Lib.; RCF.
2. For Lieutenant Dawson see **[54]**, note 2.

Illustration Plate 4

[61] ROBERT K. DAWSON   (Large)   **London**   **1837**

NORWICH[1]   175 x 160 mm.

A Scale of 4 inches (102 mm.) to 1 Mile   1:15840

Source
The same as that of Dawson's smaller plan **[60]**.

Description
This coloured much larger plan, occupying the lower part of the plate, complements the smaller one, in that it identifies the eight wards in the central area. It shows the parish boundaries and extends beyond the old city sufficiently to show the names and position of the outer hamlets, but does not extend to the outer boundary. Below the plan is the scale.

1. Examples as for **[60]**.

Illustration Plate 4

[62] ORDNANCE SURVEY   **London**   **1838**

NORWICH[1]   325 x 480 mm.

A Scale of One Inch (25 mm.) to a Statute Mile   1:63360

Source
The first edition of the one inch to a mile Old Series Ordnance Survey map of that part of the county of Norfolk to include Norwich. National sheet number 66 was published in four quarterly

sections; the city of Norwich occupies the lower left corner of the north east section, with a tiny area of land to the north of the river near Harford Bridges on the south east section.

Outside the border of both, top right, is the sheet number in roman numerals *N°. LXVI* Top left are the individual sheet titles *N.E. (Norwich)* and *S.E. (Norwich)* respectively. Below the bottom border are the imprints *Sold by Ja^S. Gardner, Agent for the Sale of the Ordnance Maps, 163, Regent Street London,*[2] and *Engraved in the Tower of London at the ORDNANCE MAP OFFICE. The Outline by E. George* [S.E. section *A. Baker]* , *The Writing by J.W. Froggett, the Hills by J. Baker* [S.E.Section *J. Caplin*], *& Published by Colonel Colby F.R.S. L.& E. M.R.I.A., &c. Jany. 1st.1838.*[3]

Origin of the Plan

The city of Norwich was first surveyed on a scale of 2 inches to a mile in 1817. When Colby became Superintendent in 1820 he came to the conclusion that much of the work which had been carried out, but had not yet been published, was so inaccurate as to require systematic revision. The plan of Norwich itself was completely revised in 1836, and, incorporated with the revised surveys of the adjoining areas, was finally approved for publication in 1838.[4]

Description

Sheet LXVI NE extends north to Buxton, and east to beyond Acle; Norwich is towards the south west corner of the Sheet. The map is finely engraved, and set the standard for many years ahead. In one respect the map was ahead of its time, as it shows by way of faint double pecked line the projected Eastern Counties Railway from the south, and on towards Yarmouth.[5] The map has a wide border of an outer thin and inner thick line, and inside these lines a 'piano key' border on all four sides, within which are printed the degrees of latitude and longitude. Outside the bottom border, in addition to the imprints, is the scale. Sheet LXVI SE, which includes a very small part of the city within its outer southern boundary; is in layout similar to Sheet LXVI NE.

Later History

The later history of the One Inch Old Series Ordnance Survey maps is a story on its own, and is beyond the scope of this work. The maps were frequently revised, particularly necessary in order to take account of the development of the railways, and were increasingly used as the basis of maps by commercial publishers.

1.Not in Stephen. Royal Geographical Society ; BL Maps C9.a.2 (state 2 of Sheet 66 NE, and state 1 of Sheet 66 SE). Later states, Nfk.Lib.and RCF. The original surveyors drawings of 1817 (Sheet 241), and 1836 (part of Sheet 66), are in the BL, Maps.
2. James Gardner succeeded William Faden as Agent for the sale of Ordnance Survey maps in 1823; he retired in 1840, when his imprint was deleted. .
3. Thomas Frederick Colby , 1784-1852, officer of the Royal Engineers, Superintendent of the Ordnance Survey from 1820 (appointed as Major) until 1847 (appointed Major-General).
4. For details of the work of the Ordnance Survey in the area, and the printing and publication of Sheet 66 see the Introduction by J.B.Harley to *The Old Series of Ordnance Survey Maps of England and Wales Volume V*, Lympne Castle, 1987, and the Notes by J.B.Harley to the Reprint of the First Edition of the Survey by David & Charles, Newton Abbot, 1970 - their sheet 46, covering O.S. Sheet 66.
5. For the inclusion of the railway see William Ionn [59], note 3.

SELECT BIBLIOGRAPHY

Bendall, S. *Dictionary of Land Surveyors and Mapmakers...1530-1850*, 2nd. ed., London, 1997.
Blomefield, F. *The History of the City and County of Norwich Vols. I and II*, London, 1806.
Carroll, R.A. *Printed Maps of Lincolnshire 1576-1900*, Lincoln, 1996.
Chubb, T. *The Printed Maps in the Atlases of Great Britain ..1579-1870*, London, 1927.
Chubb, T. *A Descriptive List of the Printed Maps of Norfolk 1574-1919*, and Stephen, G.A. *A Descriptive List of Norwich Plans 1541-1914*, Norwich, 1928.
Cozens-Hardy, B. and Kent, E.A. *The Mayors of Norwich 1408-1835*, Norwich, 1938.
Darlington, I and Howgego, J. *Printed Maps of London, c.1553-1850*, London, 1964.
Delano-Smith, C. and Kain, R.J.P. *English Maps : A History*, London, 1999.
Elliott, J. *The City in Maps*, London, 1987.
Fordham, A. *Town Plans of the British Isles*, London, 1965.
Gough, R. *British Topography*, London, 1780.
Harley, J.B. *The Old Series Ordnance Survey Maps of England Wales Volume V*, Lympne Castle, 1987.
Harvey P.D.A. *Maps in Tudor England*, London, 1993.
Hodson, D. *County Atlases of the British Isles Published after 1703 Volume I*, Tewin, 1984.
Hodson, D. - do - *Volume II*, Tewin, 1988.
Hodson, D. - do - *Volume III*, London, 1997.
Hudson, W. and Tingey, J.C. *The Records of the City of Norwich*, Norwich 1906.
Kirkpatrick J. (Ed. Hudson, W.)*The Streets and Lanes of the City of Norwich*, Norwich, 1889.
Koeman, C. *Atlantes Neerlandici*, Amsterdam, 1967-1970.
Maxted, I. *The London Book Trades 1775-1800*, Folkestone, 1977.
Moreland, C. and Bannister D. *Antique Maps*, 2nd ed. , London, 1986.
Shirley, R.W. *County Atlases of the British Isles...1579-1703*, London, 1970.
Shirley, R.W. *Printed Maps of the British Isles 1650-1750*, Tring, 1988.
Skelton, R.A. *County Atlases of the British Isles...1579-1703*, London, 1970.
Smith, D. *Antique Maps of the British Isles*, London, 1982.
Tooley, R.V. *Dictionary of Mapmakers*, Tring, 1972.
Tooley's Dictionary of Mapmakers Revised Edition A-D, Tring, 1999.
Tyacke, S. *London Map-sellers*, Tring, 1978.
Upcott, W. *A Bibliographical Account of the Principal Works relating to English Topography,* London, 1818.
Woodward S. *The Norfolk Topographer's Manual*, London, 1842.

INDEX

The numbers in Bold Type are the identification numbers of the Plans in the text, and follow in the Index the relevant page numbers. Illustrations are not separately indexed, but are found either on the same page as the description of the Plan to which they relate, or on an adjacent page.

Amsterdam 6, 9, 10,11
Antwerp 12
Armstrong A. 55(n)
Armstrong M.J. 55
Armstrong, Marcus 57, **[42]**, 44(n)

Barker H.A. xii, 66, **[49]**
Basssett and Chiswell 18
Beauties of England and Wales 54, 65, 67
Beer J.C. 19, **[15]**
Bettes, John 1, 4(n)
bird's eye views ix, 8, 9, 10, 11, 12
Bleau W.J. 12
Blomefield, F xi, 44, **[33]**, 45, 63, **[47]**
Bodleian vii, x
Booth, M. 50, 52, 53, **[38]**, 55
boundaries x, xii(n), 71, 75, 76
Bowen, Emanuel 39
Braun, Georg xi, 4, **[2]**, 7, 8, 14, 68
British Atlas 65
British Library vii, x
Buck, S. and N. xii, 42, **[31]**, 44, **[32]**, 49, 54, 62

Castle Museum vii, 67(n)
Chase W. 27, 25, 33(n), 35, 39, **[28]**, 40, 59
Chubb, Thomas ix
Cleer, T. xi, 20, **[16]**, 23, **[17]**, 27, 36
Cole, G xii, 54, 63, **[48]**, 64, 66
Corbridge, J. xi, 33(n), 36, **[26]**, 38
Coronelli V. xi, 23, **[18]**, 24, **[19]**
Creighton, R. xii, 76, **[58]**
Cross-Grove, H. 34
Crouse, J. 52, 53, 55
Cuningham, W. i, ix, xi, 1, **[1]**, 4, 8, 19, 68

Dallinger, J. 70
Dawson, R.K. xi, 71, **[54]**, 77, **[60]**, 78, **[61]**

Day, John 1, 3(n)
Dicey C. & Co. 17, 18, 53, **[39]**
Dodsley R. 49

Elizabeth I, progress 3, 5
Elstrack, R. 8

Faden, W. xii(n), 79(n)
Foster, G. 33(n), 40, **[29]**
Foster, Elizabeth 41
Frankfurt-am-Main 13

Gardner J. 79
Goadby, R. 44, 54, **[40]**, 62
Goddard T. 27, 33(n), 39, **[28]**, 40, 41, **[30]**
Goodman, R. 33(n), 41, **[30]**
Gough, Richard x
Guide To Knowledge 73

Harris, J. 36, 38(n)
Hermannides R. 15, **[10]**, 19, 24
Hinton, J. 44, 47, 48, **[34]**
Hochstetter, Anthony xi, 59, **[44]**, 60
Hoefnagel, Joris 5, 6(n)
Hogenberg, Frans xi. 4, **[2]**, 6(n), 7, 8, 14
Holinshed, R. 4(n)
Hondius, Henricus 10
Hondius, J. (Senior) 9(n)
Hondius, J. (Junior) 9, **[5]**, 10, 11, **[7]**
Hoyle J. xi, 27, **[21]**

Index Monasticus 17, 18
Ionn, W. xii, 77, **[59]**

Kemp, G. 75, **[57]**, 76(n)
Kirkall, E. 33(n)
Kirkpatrick, J. x, 4(n), 29, 31(n), 33
Kirkpatrick, T. xii, 29, **[22]**, 33, **[23]**, 34, 35, 39, 53

King, S. xi, 50, **[36]**, 52, **[37]**, 55, 61

Lea, Philip 17
Löffler J.E. 15(n)
London xii(n)

Manning, J. ix, xi, xii, 61, 68, **[53]**, 72, 73, **[55]**
manuscript maps xii(n)
Meisner, D. 13, **[9]**
Millard, W.S. ix, xi, 61, 68, **[53]**
Middleburgh 16,
Münster, Samuel xi

Nichols J.B. 75, **[57]**, 76(n)
Nicholls, S. xi, 25, **[20]**, 26
Ninham, H. 33, 62(n), 73(n)
Newcastle-upon-Tyne, 36
Norfolk, Duke of 20, 23(n), 38(n)
Norfolk Heritage Centre vii
Norfolk, maps x, 6, 16, 38, 39, 41, 40, 65
Norwich Directory 55, 59, 62
Norwich Gazette 27(n), 34, **[24]**, 36
Norwich Mercury 35, **[25]**
Nuremberg 14, 19

Overton J. 16
Ordnance Survey ix, xii(n), 71, 78, **[62]**

Padua 8
Panoramania 66
Parkin, C. 46, 48
Pinnock W, xii, 73, **[56]**
Peck T. 59(n), 62
Political Magazine 61, **[45]**
Poole, W. 63

railways ix, 77, 79
Roades, W. 40, 41
Rose, George 20(n)
Rotterdam 16
Rowlandson, Thomas xii(n)
Ryland J. 44, 49, **[35]**, 54, 62

Sanctuary Map xii(n), 1
Savanarola, R. 8
Saxton, C. ix, 16, **[12]**
Sayer, Robert 41, 42
Smith, T. xi, 58, 59, **[43]**
Smith, William 8, 9(n)
Speed, J. x, xi, 8, **[4]**, 10, 11, 15, 17, **[13]**
Starling T. 66, **[50]**
Stent, P. 16, **[11]**, 18
Stephen, George ix

Taylor, Richard 67, **[51]**, 68, **[52]**
Thompson J. xi, 55, **[41]**, 56
Topographical Dictionary 76

Universal Magazine 48

Valezo, Francisco 7, **[3]**, 25
Verbiest, P. i, 10, 12, **[8]**
Venice 7, 8, 23, 24
Visscher C.J 10, **[6]**

Waesberge J. van 5
Walton, R. 10, 18, **[14]**

NOTES